Complete Handbook of
INDOOR and OUTDOOR GAMES and ACTIVITIES
for Young Children

Jean R. Feldman, Ph.D.

Illustrations by
Rebecca Feldman Foster

**THE CENTER FOR APPLIED
RESEARCH IN EDUCATION**
West Nyack, New York 10995

Library of Congress Cataloging-in-Publication Data

Feldman, Jean R., 1947–.
    Complete handbook of indoor & outdoor games & activities for young
children / Jean Feldman ; illustrations by Rebecca Feldman Foster.
        p.   cm.
    ISBN 0-87628-119-6
    1. Early childhood education—Activity programs—Handbooks,
manuals, etc.   2. Educational games—Handbooks, manuals, etc.
I. Title.
LB1139.35.A37F45   1994   94-15861
790.1'922—dc20   CIP

Printed in the United States of America

10   9   8   7   6   5   4   3

ISBN 0-87628-119-6

**THE CENTER FOR APPLIED RESEARCH
IN EDUCATION**
West Nyack, NY 10994
A Simon & Schuster Company

On the World Wide Web at http://www.phdirect.com

Prentice-Hall International (UK) Limited, *London*
Prentice-Hall of Australia Pty. Limited, *Sydney*
Prentice-Hall Canada Inc., *Toronto*
Prentice-Hall Hispanoamericana, S.A., *Mexico*
Prentice-Hall of India Private Limited, *New Delhi*
Prentice-Hall of Japan, Inc., *Tokyo*
Simon & Schuster Asia Pte. Ltd., *Singapore*
Editora Prentice-Hall do Brasil, Ltda., *Rio de Janeiro*

This book is dedicated to
my children, Holly and Nick.

ABOUT THE AUTHOR

Jean Feldman has been a teacher in the Atlanta area for over 25 years. Currently she is an instructor in the Early Childhood Department at DeKalb Technical Institute. Dr. Feldman has a B.A. from the University of Georgia, a D.A.S.T. from Emory University, and a M.A. and Ph.D. from Georgia State University. She is a member of the National Association for the Education of Young Children, Georgia Association for Young Children, and the Georgia Preschool Association. Dr. Feldman presents to professional groups across the country and serves on the board of several organizations. She is author of *A Survival Guide for Preschool Teachers* (The Center for Applied Research in Education, 1991), *Kids Atlanta,* and other materials for teachers. She is married and the mother of two teenagers.

COME AND PLAY!

Why?

The activities in this book are based on the simple premise that children learn more when they're having fun. They also capitalize on children's need to learn through hands-on experiences. When children are playing games, their interest and motivation work together to create a wonderful learning opportunity.

The games and activities in this book will enrich your curriculum and enhance the children's development in the following areas:

- Intellectually . . . thinking skills, language development, problem solving, math concepts, creativity
- Socially . . . . cooperation, sharing, friendship, belonging to a group
- Emotionally . . . . independence, confidence, self-esteem
- Physically . . . . . . large- and small-motor development, body awareness, stress release

Learning need not be confined to workbooks and the four walls of the classroom, but should flow outside on the playground and be integrated throughout the day. Take advantage of the different seasons, your outdoor environment, and the "teachable moment" in implementing the ideas in this book.

The following symbols help designate the appropriate environment for each activity:

Indicates a game or activity to use inside the classroom.

Suggests an activity to use outdoors.

Shows an activity that can be used inside or outside.

Who?

At all stages we must be sensitive to children's unique development and adapt activities to fit their needs and interests. There is a broad range of ages provided for in this book to allow you to pick and choose what is just right for your particular group. Activities and games should always be fun and offer children a successful experience. Children should be encouraged to make choices, experiment, and "discover" on their own. Learning proceeds from the inside out, and these tools and materials will spark children's curiosity and get them involved actively in the learning process.

Remember! Adapt, change, simplify, or make the games more complex to meet the specific needs of the children in your classroom.

How?

Games are a natural vehicle for integrating concepts and reinforcing skills. A real advantage of teacher-made games is that you can adapt them to meet your goals and objectives. For example, if your students are interested in dinosaurs, then create a game with dinosaurs and bones; when you are doing a unit on the wild west, create one with ponies and saddles; if a child is only interested in sports, then let it be a baseball or football game. Whatever skill or concept you are working on can be introduced or extended with an activity in this book. From shapes, to colors, letters, words, and math facts, personalize the games to fit your curriculum and your children's interests.

What?

These basic materials will make game construction a breeze:

construction paper	markers
crayons	scissors
posterboard	tissue paper
file folders	rubber cement
brass fasteners	stapler
hole punch	tape
envelopes	craft sticks
self-lock bags	paper plates
lunch bags	library pockets
clear self-stick vinyl or laminating machine	paper clips

Games are also a great way to recycle materials you often throw away. Start saving some of the items below, or ask your parents to save them for you:

cardboard food boxes	cigar boxes
file containers	shoe boxes
newspapers	magazines

coupons
catalogs
laundry detergent boxes

old toys
puzzles
paper scraps
wrapping paper scraps
plastic bottles
felt and fabric scraps
clothespins
bottle caps
junk mail
potato chip canisters
self-stick vinyl

greeting cards
old workbooks
milk jugs and cartons

wallpaper scraps
grocery bags
computer paper
food cans
buttons
cardboard rollers
hangers
margarine tubs
egg cartons
appliance boxes
stickers

Helpful Hints!

Consider these guidelines in constructing games and activities for your class:

1. Limit games and activities to one concept or skill.
2. Keep games short.
3. Make games colorful and attractive. Laminate or cover with clear self-stick vinyl to make games last longer.
4. Construct self-contained games for easy care and clean-up.
5. Try to make games where all children will be winners and feel successful. Emphasize the fun of playing, rather than winning or losing.
6. Give simple directions and clear rules.
7. Give children many different types of games and activities from which to choose. Provide children with games they can play individually, in small groups, and in large groups.
8. Encourage children to be persistent and complete games and activities. Give them positive reinforcement when they play games and follow through on activities.
9. Demonstrate how to use the games before you set them out. Play with the children at first, then move outside of the game as they become more familiar with the rules.
10. Observe the children, then adapt the games and rules to their needs and interests.

11. Swap games with other teachers.

12. Ask parents to help you make games at home or have a game workshop for parents one evening or Saturday.

13. Set up a system where children can "check out" games to take home and play with their parents or siblings.

14. Rotate games and continually add new ones to keep the children's interest. Observe them to see which format they particularly enjoy.

15. Use games as an assessment tool. Make anecdotal records as you observe the children playing games, then use this information to help you plan and give them meaningful experiences.

Where?

Put games in the content areas where they belong, such as math games in the math center, or reading games in the language arts center. Games can be hung on a clothesline with clothespins, attached to a bulletin board with tacks, mounted on the back of a shelf or door, hung on the wall, stored in shoe racks, or taped to the floor. Use your imagination!

Plastic tubs, lunchroom trays, shoe boxes, detergent boxes, coffee cans, shirt boxes, self-lock bags, paper bags, or clasp envelopes can all be used for storing games. Use self-lock sandwich bags, library pockets, envelopes, or margarine tubs to store game pieces.

So, invite your youngsters to "come and play." A lot of learning and fun will take place!

Jean Feldman

CONTENTS

Section 3: SCIENCE SURPRISES

Section 4: ARTS AND CRAFTS

Section 5: WATER, SAND, AND BLOCK PLAY 167

Section 6: DRAMATIC PLAY 187

Section 7: MOTOR SKILLS AND HOMEMADE EQUIPMENT 199

Section 8: GROUP GAMES   225

Section 9: SUPER SNACKS AND SILLY SONGS   269

Section 10: SPECIAL DAYS 287

RESOURCES 303

Language Games and Ideas

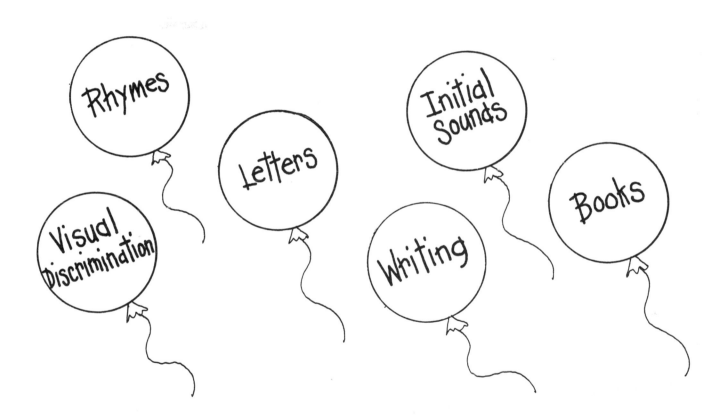

Learning to read and write will be a joy with these games and activities. There are ideas for making books, creating a writing center, extending stories, as well as exciting ways to help children love to read while giving them the skills they need to be successful.

BOO BOOS

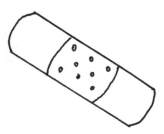

Skill: visual matching

Materials:
* assorted adhesive bandages (two of each kind)
* file folder
* self-locking plastic bag

Directions:
1. Unwrap adhesive bandages. Take one of each kind and apply to the file folder.
2. Place the remaining adhesive bandages in the plastic bag.
3. Ask the children to match the adhesive bandage in the bag to the bandaid on the file folder.

Adaptations:

* For older children, write antonyms, math facts, rhyming words, upper- and lower-case letters, and so forth, on the bandaids for them to match.
* Give each child an adhesive bandage. Ask the children to take it and place it somewhere on their body. Then have each child make up a story about how he or she got that "boo boo." Younger children can dictate a story or tell a story with the tape recorder, while older children can write their own story.

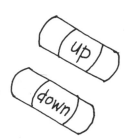

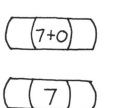

LABELS AND LOGOS

Skill: reading; visual discrimination

Materials:
* labels from food containers, store sacks, fast food restaurants, paper products, clothing, and so forth (two of each)
* 5" × 8" cardboard rectangles
* scissors, glue

Directions:

1. Cut out two of each label.
2. Glue the labels to the cardboard.
3. Take one of each label and place it on the floor or table. Give the other cards to the children and ask them to match like cards.
4. Read the words on the products together.

Adaptations:
* Let children match labels with the actual food containers.
* Make a "bag book" of sacks from restaurants and stores. Take large paper grocery sacks and cut them apart to make the pages for the book. Glue one sack to each page, then put the pages together with yarn or book rings. "Read" the book together. (The bag book provides for immediate success and makes children feel like they can read.)

3

GINGERBREAD KIDS

Skill:	visual discrimination
Materials:	* brown construction paper
	* scissors, markers, glue
	* file folder
	* envelope

Directions:

1. Cut out 16 gingerbread kids from the brown construction paper. (See the sample pattern below.)
2. With markers, make two of each kid exactly the same. (You can change their mouths, noses, number of buttons, and so forth.)
3. Glue one of each kid to the file folder.
4. Glue the envelope to the back of the folder for storing the other gingerbread kids.
5. Have the children take the gingerbread kids and match those that are alike.

Adaptation:

* Gingerbread kids can be used for making sets, matching colors, letters, sets and numerals, and so on.

© 1994 by The Center for Applied Research in Education

Gingerbread Pattern

PICTURE THIS!

Skill: visual discrimination

Materials:
* school photo or small picture of each child
* copy machine
* rubber cement
* scissors
* construction paper

Directions:
1. Glue all the photos of the children to one or two pages and make 25 copies.
2. Cut out the children's individual photos and use them for classroom labels, matching activities, games, writing, and art projects. Here are some examples.

  **Matching Lotto Game**

Concentration

 **Name Puzzles**

Name Recognition

 Bookmark **Labels**

 **Art Collage**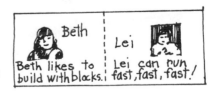

Class Books

  Classroom Helpers

Sorting and Counting

SILLY SOCKS

Skill: visual discrimination

Materials:
* construction paper (all colors), wallpaper, or fabric scraps
* scissors
* markers

Directions:
1. Using the sock pattern below, cut out a pair (two) of socks from different colors of construction paper, wallpaper, or the fabric scraps. (Fabric scraps will need to be glued to tagboard to make them firmer.) You will need as many pairs of socks as you have children in your classroom.
2. Have the children sit in a circle and close their eyes.
3. Take one of each pair of socks and "hide it" somewhere in the room in plain sight.
4. Tell the children to open their eyes. Give each child a sock, then have them hunt around the room until they find their matching silly sock. The children should return to the circle and sit down when they find their matching pair.

Adaptations:

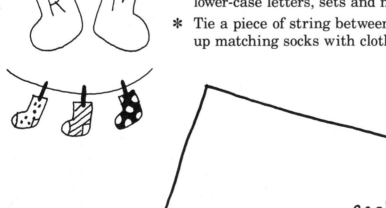

* Let the children decorate matching socks with crayons or markers, then use them for the game.
* Make other matching games with the socks, such as upper- and lower-case letters, sets and numerals, and so on.
* Tie a piece of string between two chairs and let the children hang up matching socks with clothespins.

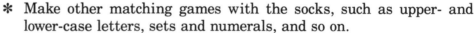

sock
Pattern

 **BOLT BOARDS**

Skill:	visual discrimination
Materials:	* fabric bolts (which you can obtain free from cloth shops) * construction paper * scissors, glue
Directions:	1. Cut different shapes from colored construction paper. (Cut two of each shape.) 2. Glue one shape to the fabric bolt. 3. Ask the children to match like shapes.

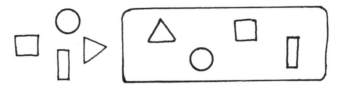

Adaptations:

* Make matching games with Old Maid cards, small cereal boxes, stickers, coupons, and so on.

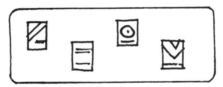

* Cut two of different textures (wallpaper, sandpaper, felt, silk, fur, aluminum foil) for the children to match.

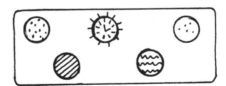

* Trace around the outline of common classroom objects on a bolt, then let children try to identify the shapes and match objects.

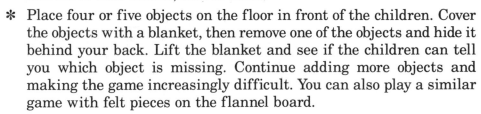

CONCENTRATION

Skill: visual memory

Materials:
* 10–30 pieces of cardboard cut in 3" squares
* stickers, stamps, or markers

Directions:

1. Take ten pieces of cardboard and put like stickers, stamps, or draw like pictures or shapes on two cards.
2. Place the cards face down on the floor or on a table.
3. One at a time, let the children turn over two cards. If the cards match, then they may keep the pair and have another turn. If the cards do not match, then the next person may turn two cards over. Children must use their visual memory skills to try and remember where matching pairs are located.
4. The game continues until all cards have been matched. The person with the most pairs wins.

Adaptations:

* Start with ten cards, then increase the amount as children become more successful.
* Make holiday and seasonal games with stickers.
* Use this game to match rhyming words, sets and numerals, upper- and lower-case letters, and so forth.
* Place four or five objects on the floor in front of the children. Cover the objects with a blanket, then remove one of the objects and hide it behind your back. Lift the blanket and see if the children can tell you which object is missing. Continue adding more objects and making the game increasingly difficult. You can also play a similar game with felt pieces on the flannel board.
* Use regular playing cards or Old Maid cards to play Concentration.

LOLLIPOPS

Skill: color recognition

Materials:
* craft sticks
* glue, scissors
* construction paper (red, blue, yellow, green, orange, and purple)
* coffee can

Directions:

1. Cut 3" circles from the construction paper. Make three or four of each color.
2. Glue a craft stick to the end of each circle to make "lollipops."
3. Have the children sit in a circle. One child is "it" and skips around the circle holding the can of lollipops while the other children sing.

Tune: *Skip to My Lou*

Lollipops, lollipops, yum, yum, yum.
Lollipops, lollipops, yum, yum, yum.
Lollipops, lollipops, yum, yum, yum.
Please come over and give me some.

"It" stops in front of one classmate who closes his or her eyes, reaches in the can, and pulls out a lollipop. If he or she can name the color, then that child may take a turn being "it."

4. Continue until each child has had a turn and has a lollipop.

Adaptations:

* Let the children sort lollipops by color.
* Play a listening game with the lollipops. Give each child a lollipop. Then say, "If you have a red one, stand up and turn around; if you have a blue one, stand up and jump three times; if you have a yellow one, stand up and shout 'hooray,'" and so on.
* Have the children use their lollipops to do addition and subtraction problems.
* Let the children color their own lollipops with crayons. Mix ¼ cup Epsom salt with ¼ cup hot water. Paint this solution on lollipops, allow to dry, and your lollipops will look "sugary."

MOMMAS AND BABIES

Skill: color matching

Materials:
* construction paper (eight basic colors)
* scissors
* storage bag or envelope

Directions:
1. Cut out eight momma bears from construction paper using the pattern below.
2. Cut out eight baby bears from construction paper using the pattern below.
3. Children match baby bears and momma bears by like colors.
4. Store pieces in plastic storage bag or envelope.

Adaptation:
* Upper- and lower-case letters, sets and numerals, beginning consonant sounds, number words, and other skills can be practiced with this game.

Large Bear Pattern

Small Bear Pattern

 HOT DOG!

Skill: color matching

Materials:
* construction paper (eight basic colors)
* scissors
* envelope or plastic bag

Directions:
1. Cut out eight hot dogs and eight buns from different colors of construction paper using the patterns below.
2. Spread out hot dog buns. Ask the children to match up hot dogs with their matching buns.

Adaptations:
* Make a file folder game with these patterns.
* Use the hot dogs and buns to reinforce contractions and to make alternative matching games.

11

SCOOP AND RHYME

Skill: rhyming words

Materials:
* construction paper
* scissors, glue, envelope
* rhyming pictures

Directions:
1. Cut out eight cones and eight scoops of ice cream using the patterns.
2. Copy the rhyming pictures on the following page.
3. Glue matching pictures on scoops and cones.
4. Mix up the pieces, then ask the children to put rhyming pairs together.
5. Store pieces in an envelope.

Adaptation:
* Scoops and cones can be used to match sets and numerals, math facts, or upper- and lower-case letters.

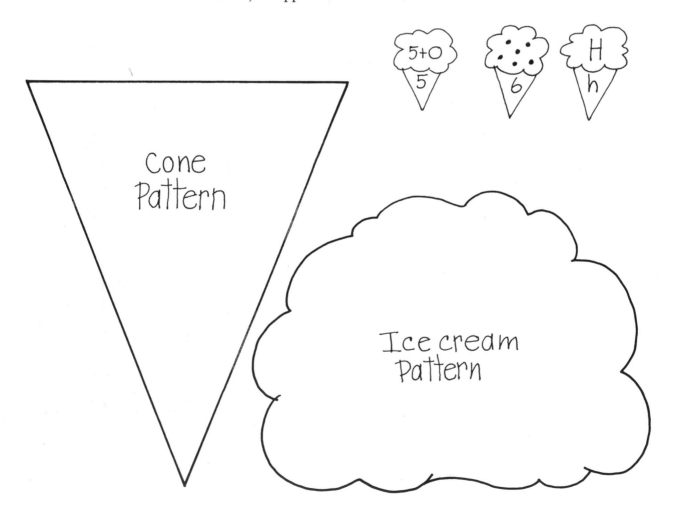

Cone Pattern

Ice cream Pattern

PICTURES FOR "SCOOP AND RHYME"

Bat	Hat	Star	Car
Moon	Spoon	Cake	Rake
Tree	Bee	Sock	Clock
House	Mouse	Pan	Man

13

PUZZLE PAIRS

Skill: rhyming words

Materials:
* cardboard, tagboard, or construction paper cut in 4" × 7" pieces
* markers
* scissors

Directions:
1. Take five pieces of cardboard. On each rectangle draw two rhyming pictures, or use the pictures from "Scoop and Rhyme."
2. Cut a puzzle shape through the middle of each card between the two rhyming pictures.
3. Mix up all the pieces, then let the children match the pictures that rhyme. This is self-checking, for the puzzle will fit if the children are correct.

Adaptations:
* Make similar games for matching shapes, colors, textures, upper- and lower-case letters, pictures and beginning sounds, opposites, math facts, contractions, and so forth.
* Vary the number of cards in the game depending on the ability of the children.
* Use paper plates or 4" × 6" index cards to make puzzle pairs.

WIGGLE WORMS

Skill: letter recognition

Materials:
- * empty can (select one with a smooth edge, such as a drink mix can or potato chip canister)
- * cardboard
- * glue, paper, markers

Directions:

1. Cover the outside of the can with paper. Write "wiggle worms" on it and decorate with worms.
2. Cut the cardboard into 30 rectangles that will fit in your can. (2½" × 5" usually works well.)
3. On the bottom of 26 cards, print the letters of the alphabet. On the other four cards draw a "wiggle worm."
4. Place the cards in the can.
5. Have the children sit in a circle. One at a time, have the children take the worm can, pull out a card, and identify the letter on the bottom of the card. If there is a worm on the bottom of the card, the child yells "wiggle worms" and everyone should stand up and "wiggle like a worm."
6. Continue passing the can around until all the cards are gone or you run out of time.

Adaptations:
- * This game can be adapted to reinforce shapes, colors, sets, numerals, sight words, math facts, or anything else that you are working on in your classroom.
- * Let the children play this game in small groups or take home to play with their parents.

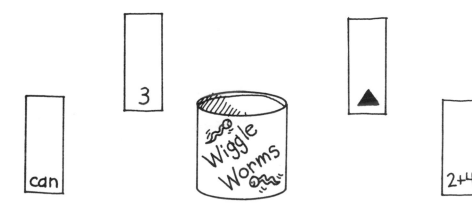

15

RUBOVER

Skill: letter recognition; sight words

Materials:
* school glue
* cardboard (5" × 8" rectangles)
* paper, crayons

Directions:
1. Print the letters or words you are working on with glue on the cardboard. Dry.
2. Give the cards to the children and let them feel the letters or words with their hands.
3. Put a card on the table, cover it with a sheet of paper, then rub with a crayon. Just like magic, the letter or word will appear.

Adaptations:

* Put food coloring in the glue.
* For younger children, tape the cards to the table to keep them in place.
* Make rubovers of numerals, shapes, animals, or seasonal objects.
* Sprinkle glitter or sand on the glue when it is wet to give it more texture.
* Make rubovers of each child's name.

ALPHABET WALK

A B C D

Skill:　　　　letters and sounds

Materials:　　* a pretty day

Directions:

1. Tell the children that you are going to take them on an alphabet walk where they will look for things that begin with different letters of the alphabet.

2. Go outside and find something that starts with "a" (*examples:* ant, acorn); "b" (*examples:* bird, ball), and so forth.

Adaptations:

* As a follow-up, make a language experience chart of the letters and objects.

* Divide older children into groups and give them different letters. Ask them to make a list of all the things they could find that start with the sound.

* Give each child a sheet with a different letter on it and ask them to go outside and draw a picture of something in nature beginning with the sound. (Sometimes you have to use your imagination!) Put the pages together to make "Our Nature ABC Book."

17

COOKING UP SOME LETTERS

Skill: letter recognition; alphabetical order

Materials:
* magnetic letters
* metal cookie sheet

Directions:

1. Ask the children to identify magnetic letters as they put them on the cookie sheet.
2. See if they can put them in alphabetical order. (You might want to pair children to do this activity.)

Adaptations:

* Give children flashcards of simple sight words to reproduce with the magnetic letters.
* Make story characters from construction paper and attach a strip of magnetic tape to the back. Use the cookie sheet like a flannel board to tell the story. (This is particularly fun to do with the story about the Gingerbread Boy.)
* Give children play dough or clay to form into letters on the cookie sheet.
* Let children make letters from frozen bread dough. Then cook and eat.

BEANBAG TOSS

s	l	f
m	d	r
p	t	v

Skill: letter recognition

Materials:
- ∗ beanbags
- ∗ posterboard
- ∗ markers, yardstick

Directions:

1. Divide posterboard into nine sections.
2. Print a different letter in each section.
3. Have the children stand behind a designated line and toss the beanbag.
4. Ask them to identify the letter where the beanbag lands. (Some may also be able to think of a word that begins with each sound.)

Adaptations:

- ∗ Make a similar game for reinforcing colors, numerals, shapes, or words.
- ∗ Use chalk outside on the sidewalk to make a beanbag toss game.
- ∗ Write numerals in the sections, then give each child two beanbags to toss. They can add up the numerals and keep their own score.

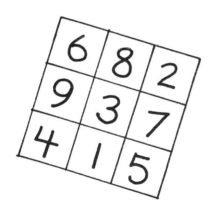

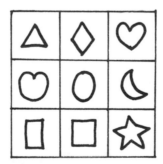

SKUNK'S HOLE

Skill: letter recognition

Materials:
* plastic milk jug
* posterboard
* markers, scissors, glue
* green tissue paper or construction paper

Directions:
1. Cut a 4½" circle in one side of the milk jug as shown.
2. Color the milk jug with markers to look like a tree. Glue green construction paper or tissue paper leaves to the top.
3. Cut posterboard into 3" squares. On 26 squares print the letters of the alphabet. Photocopy the skunk below and glue it to the four remaining cards.
4. Mix all the cards and put them face down inside the bottom of the milk jug.
5. One at a time, children draw a card and try to identify the letter on their card. If a skunk is drawn, the child is out of the game.

Adaptation:
* Use this game for color, shape, numeral, or sight word reinforcement.

CRASH CARS

Skill: letter recognition

Materials:
* cardboard
* scissors
* markers

Directions:
1. Cut out 30 cars from cardboard using the pattern below.
2. Print a letter on each car. On four cars write the word "crash."
3. Mix up the cars and place them face down on the floor or table. One at a time, children draw a car and identify the letter on it. They may keep the car if they are correct. If they pick the "crash car," they must return their other cars to the bottom of the pile.

Adaptation:
* Use this game format for reinforcing sight words, numerals, colors, and so forth.

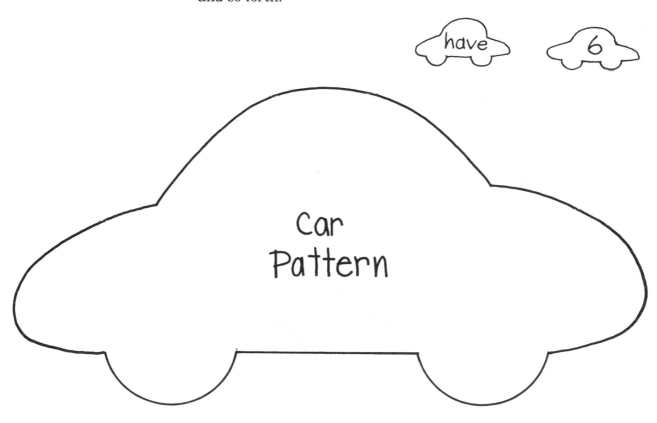

Car Pattern

ALPHABET SOUP

Skill: letter recognition

Materials:
* vegetable soup can
* cardboard cut in 2" squares
* markers
* cloth tape

Directions:

1. Clean out the inside of the soup can. Put cloth tape around the open edge so it won't cut the children.
2. Print alphabet letters on the cardboard squares with markers.
3. Put the cardboard squares in the soup can. Have the children sit in a circle. Pass the can around, asking each child to select a letter and name his or her letter.
4. Let each child think of something that begins with his or her letter or act out something beginning with the letter.

Adaptations:

* More advanced children can put the letters in alphabetical order.
* Older children could think of a particular part of speech, such as a verb, adjective, or noun beginning with their letter.
* Let the children try to spell words with the different letters in the can. (Make several squares with vowels and letters that are frequently used.)
* Give the children cereal or pasta in the shape of letters for them to identify or make words.
* Let the children make letters with their bodies.

APPLES AND WORMS

Skill:	matching upper- and lower-case letters
Materials:	* construction paper (red and yellow)
	* scissors, markers
	* storage bag or envelope
Directions:	1. Cut apples from red paper and worms from yellow paper. (See the patterns below.)
	2. Print upper-case letters on the apples and lower-case letters on the worms.
	3. Children should then match up worms with the appropriate apples.
	4. Store in a plastic bag or envelope.
Adaptations:	* Vary the number of worms and apples depending on the age of your children and the letters you are working on.
	* This game can be adapted to a file folder and used to reinforce color matching, sets and numerals, or math facts.

Apple Pattern

Worm Pattern

SCHOOL DAYS

Skill:	matching upper- and lower-case letters
Materials:	* construction paper or posterboard * scissors, markers, envelope or plastic bag
Directions:	1. Cut schoolhouses and children from the construction paper or posterboard. (The number you will need for this game will vary with the ability of your children.) 2. Print an upper-case letter on the schoolhouses, and a lower-case letter on the boys and girls. 3. Ask the children to match the boys and girls with their correct school. 4. Store pieces in an envelope or plastic bag.
Adaptation:	* Use this format for color matching, sets and numerals, initial consonant sounds, rhymes, and other skills.

PUZZLE PIECES

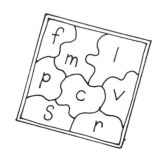

Skill: matching upper- and lower-case letters

Materials:
* commercial framed puzzle (look for these at garage sales or ask your students to bring in old ones)
* marker

Directions:

1. Take out the puzzle pieces. In each section of the frame print a lower-case letter.
2. Select one puzzle piece at a time, match it to the puzzle, then print the corresponding upper-case letter on it.
3. Have the children dump out puzzle pieces, look at the back of each piece, then match it to its corresponding letter in the frame.

Adaptation:
* This is another good self-checking game that can be used for math facts, vocabulary, and many other skills.

PONY ROUND-UP

Skill:
matching upper- and lower-case letters

Materials:
* construction paper
* markers
* scissors
* spring clothespins

Directions:
1. Trace around the horse pattern on several different colors of construction paper. Cut out. Then cut out the same number of saddles from brown construction paper.
2. Print an upper-case letter on each pony, and a lower-case letter on each saddle.
3. Let the children take each pony and stand it up using two clothespins for legs.
4. Have them put the saddle with the appropriate lower-case letter on each pony.

Adaptations:
* Let the children do this activity in the Block Center so they can build a corral to put the ponies in.
* Color matching, sets and numerals (spots on ponies), math problems, and so forth can be reinforced with this game.

Saddle Pattern (fold in half)

Pony Pattern

BATTER UP!

Skill:	initial consonant sounds
Materials:	* white posterboard
	* markers, scissors, glue, envelope or plastic bag
	* initial consonant sound pictures

Directions:

1. Cut out 20 baseballs from white posterboard using the pattern below. Draw stitching lines with markers.
2. Copy the pictures for sounds you are working on from the following pages and glue one picture to each baseball.
3. Put the balls face down on the table or floor. One at a time, children "come up to bat," turn over a baseball, and try to identify the sound that they hear at the beginning of the picture on the ball. They may keep the ball if they are correct.
4. Continue playing until all the balls are gone.
5. Store in an envelope or plastic bag.

Adaptations:

* Use baseballs to help children learn sight words or math facts.
* Write "Out" on three balls and "Homerun" on three balls. Shuffle in with the other balls, then lct the children play a card game with them by drawing a card and identifying the information on it. If they choose "Out" they lose a turn, but "Homerun" gives them an extra turn.

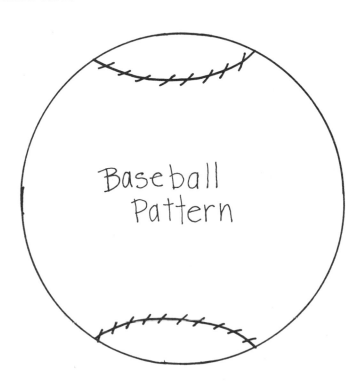

Baseball Pattern

ALPHABET PICTURES FOR "BATTER UP!"

Apple	Alligator	Book	Bear
Cat	Car	Dog	Dinosaur
Elephant	Egg	Fish	Flag
Goat	Giraffe	House	Horse

ALPHABET PICTURES FOR "BATTER UP!"

Ice Cream	Iguana	Jump Rope	Jar
Kangaroo	King	Lion	Leaf
Mitten	Mouse	Octopus	Owl
Penguin	Pig	Queen	Quilt

ALPHABET PICTURES FOR "BATTER UP!"

Ring	Rabbit	Snake	Sun
Turtle	Television	Umbrella	Unicorn
Violin	Vase	Wagon	Whale
X-ray	Yo-Yo	Yarn	Zebra

DINOSAURS AND BONES

Skill:　　　　　initial consonant sounds

Materials:
* construction paper, white posterboard
* markers, scissors, glue, envelope, or plastic bag
* initial consonant sound pictures (see "Batter Up!" activity)

Directions:
1. Cut dinosaurs from construction paper. Cut bones from white posterboard.
2. Copy initial consonant sound pictures, then glue pictures with sounds you want to reinforce on the dinosaurs. Write matching letters on the bones.
3. Children match pictures with the beginning sounds on the bones.
4. Store in an envelope or plastic bag.

Adaptation:
* Match rhyming words, pictures, or colors with this game.

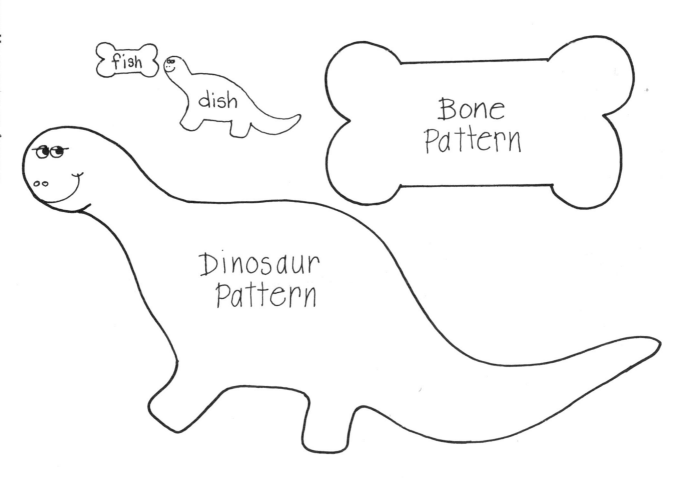

POP-UPS

Skill: initial consonant sounds

Materials:
* tagboard or heavy paper
* scissors, glue, and markers
* pictures from old workbooks of objects beginning with different consonant sounds

Directions:

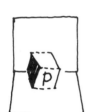

1. Cut several pop-ups out of tagboard using the pattern on the following page.
2. Fold in half. Cut in on the solid lines.
3. Take the middle flap and bend it inside.
4. Glue a picture on the front cover of the pop-up.
5. Open it up and write the beginning sound of the picture on the pop-up flap.
6. Children then take the card and try to identify the initial consonant sound of the picture on the front. The correct letter will "pop up" at them when they open the card.

Adaptations:
* Print math facts on the outside and the answer inside.
* Draw sets on the outside and print the appropriate numeral on the inside.
* Write color words, number words, or sight words on the front. Then put a picture on the inside.
* Use pop-ups to make three-dimensional art projects. Color a background, then glue characters, houses, animals, and other objects to the pop-up. (You can also make several flaps on one pop-up.)

Pop-up Pattern

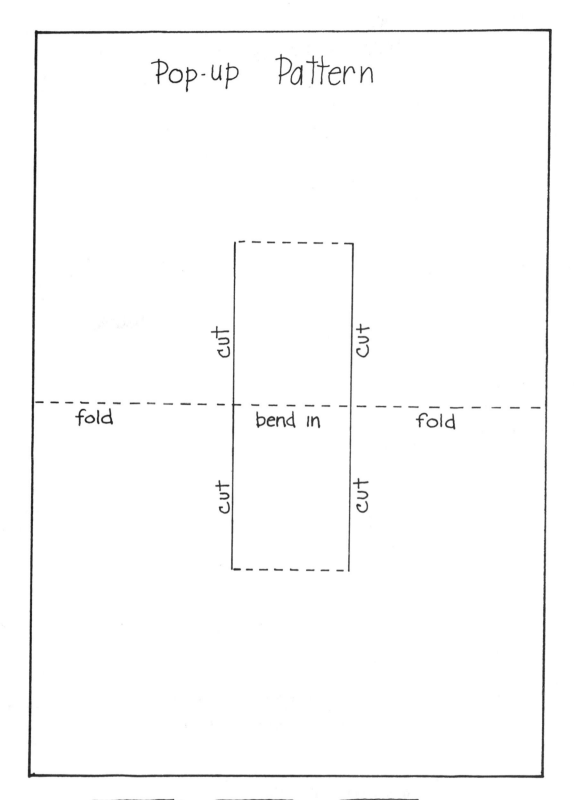

cut   cut

fold   bend in   fold

cut   cut

Fold in half. Cut in on lines.   Bend tab to inside.   Open and pop-up!

BUILDING BLOCKS FOR LEARNING

Skill: initial consonant sounds

Materials:
* unit blocks (squares and rectangles)
* tagboard or heavy paper
* markers, tape, scissors
* initial consonant sound pictures (see "Batter Up!" activity)

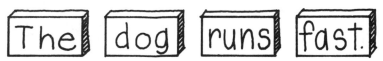

Directions:
1. Cut the paper to fit on the blocks and tape in place.
2. On the square block write the beginning consonant sound.
3. On the rectangular block write the end of the word and glue the picture.
4. Children match beginning sounds to make words.

Adaptations:
* Make similar blocks for working on blends.

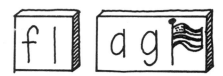

* Use blocks for building sentences.

* Match upper- and lower-case letters with blocks.

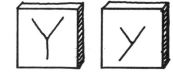

* Make word family games with blocks.

* Do math problems with blocks.

$$2 + 4 = 6$$

 **TEE TIME**

Skill: initial consonant sounds

Materials:
* 3" × 5" index cards (or cardboard cut that size)
* felt pens
* hole punch
* golf tees
* pictures of objects with initial consonant sounds (see "Batter Up!" activity)

Directions:

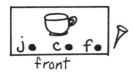

1. At the top of the index card glue a picture.
2. Make three holes along the bottom of the card and print a letter next to each hole. (One letter should be the correct answer.)
3. On the back of the card, draw a circle around the hole where the correct answer is located.
4. Children should then take the cards and insert a golf tee in the hole by the initial consonant sound for the picture on the card.
5. Turn the card over and self-check.

Adaptation:
* Use these cards for math facts, alphabetical order, sight words, and so on.

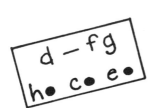
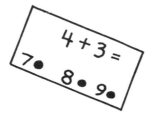

ROCK AND ROLL

Skill: initial consonant sounds

Materials:
* 16" × 24" piece of cardboard
* 24 pieces of heavy paper or construction paper cut in 4" × 6" rectangles
* markers, ruler, scissors, glue
* die
* old workbook

Directions:

1. Measure horizontal lines across the cardboard 8" apart. Trace over each line with a marker.
2. Draw a vertical line that will cut the other sections in half as shown.
3. In each section put dots from 1–6, representing the different sides of the die.
4. Take the 4" × 6" rectangles and glue a picture to the front of each one. Print the beginning consonant sound on the back.
5. Deal out four cards to each section with the picture facing up. Let the first child take the die and roll it. That child locates the section with the corresponding number of dots on it and tries to identify the beginning sound of the picture on the top card. (They can check on the back to see if they're correct.) They may keep the card if they are correct. The die is then passed to the next child who rolls it, tries to identify the beginning sound in the corresponding section, and so forth. (If there are no cards left in the section rolled, then the die goes to the next player.)
6. Continue the game until all the cards are gone. The child with the most cards wins the game.

Adaptation:
* Sight words, spelling words, math facts, and other information can be reinforced with this game.

© 1994 by The Center for Applied Research in Education

ANIMAL CRACKERS

Skill: initial consonant sounds

Materials:
* empty box of animal crackers
* plastic berry baskets
* plastic animals, animal stickers, or pictures of animals
* 2" squares of posterboard
* scissors, glue, tape

Directions:

1. Glue pictures or stickers of animals to the squares of cardboard. Store these cards or plastic animals in the cracker box.
2. Print letters to match the beginning sounds of the animals on 3" squares and tape them to the baskets.
3. Ask the children to name the animals and put them in the cage that has the same sound at the beginning of the word.

Adaptation:
* Put numerals on the baskets and ask the children to make sets with small plastic animals.

BORN TO SHOP

Skill: initial consonant sounds

Materials:
* lunch bags
* markers, scissors, glue
* toy catalogs, magazines, mail order catalogs, and so on
* construction paper cut in 3" squares

Directions:

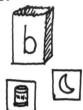

1. Take five lunch bags, and print a different consonant sound on each one.
2. Cut pictures out of the catalogs and magazines beginning with those sounds and glue them to construction paper squares.
3. Open the lunch bags. Have the children sort through the pictures, placing each one in the bag with the matching sound.

Adaptations:
* Ask children to sort pictures into food groups in a similar game.
* Have children sort objects by color into the bags.
* Print numerals on the lunch bags. Then ask the children to count out appropriate sets with counters or small food.

ALPHABET CATEGORIES

Skill: initial consonant sounds

Materials:
* two different colors of posterboard
* markers

Directions:

1. Cut each sheet of posterboard into 23 squares that are approximately 4".
2. On one color print the alphabet letters. (Print "*u* and *v*" on one card and "*x, y,* and *z*" on one card.)
3. On the other set of cards print the following categories:

something in the yard	an animal
a fruit or vegetable	a movie star
something in the kitchen	a tool
a river or lake	a town or city
a country	a machine
a type of transportation	a food
something you wear	an action
something you find in the zoo	a plant
a toy	a book
a song	a boy
a famous person	a girl
something in the school	a game
a TV show	a feeling
a color	an occupation

   (You can make these categories easier or more difficult to fit the abilities of your students.)

4. Shuffle each set of cards. Have the children sit in a circle, or divide them into teams. Draw a card from the "letter" pile and a card from the "category" pile. See who can think of something in each category that begins with the letter. The person or team may keep the card.

Adaptation:

* When introducing this game, play it as a large group activity. As children become more competent, they may enjoy playing in teams or smaller groups.

 **COLOR ME**

Skill:	color word recognition
Materials:	* construction paper (eight basic colors), white paper
	* file folder
	* scissors, markers, glue
	* envelope
Directions:	1. Cut out crayons of different colors from the construction paper.
	2. Cut out eight ovals from the white paper.
	3. Print the color words on the ovals.
	4. Glue the envelope to the back of the file folder to hold the color words.
	5. Glue the eight crayons to the inside of the file folder.
	6. Children take the color word and match it to the appropriate crayon.
Adaptations:	* Make crayons and ovals of the same color and use this game for color matching.
	* Match upper- and lower-case letters, antonyms, and so forth, with crayons and ovals.

 **FLIP BOOK**

Skill: word families

Materials:
* cardboard or heavy paper
* markers, hole punch
* metal ring

Directions:

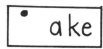

1. Cut the cardboard into a 5" × 11" rectangle. Cut five other pieces of cardboard 5" × 3".
2. On the right side of the rectangle print a word ending (*at, an, ake, ill, ot, in, ike*) as shown.
3. On the smaller cards, print consonant sounds and blends that can be added to the endings to make new words.
4. Punch holes in the top of the letter cards and attach to the left of the word ending.
5. Read the new words you make as you change the beginning sound.

Adaptations:

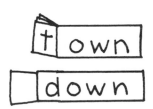

* Make flip books for other word families.
* Another version of this game can be made with an 8½" × 11" sheet of paper. Cut the paper in half lengthwise. Fold over one end approximately 3". Print a letter on the folded flap, then write the rest of the word on the remaining paper. Open the flap and print a letter that will make a rhyming word.
* Cut out large cake, hat, and ball shapes from cardboard. On a 2" × 15" strip of cardboard, print consonants as shown. Make a slit in the objects so you can slide the consonants to make new words as shown.

LOOK AND SEE

Skill: sight words

Materials:
* 5" × 7" construction paper
* glue, scissors, markers
* pictures of simple objects

Directions:

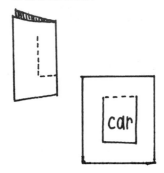

1. Take two pieces of construction paper. Fold one piece in half and cut an "L" shape starting on the fold line as shown.
2. Open up and bend the flap back at the top.
3. Glue around the edges, then apply it to the second sheet of construction paper.
4. Write a word on the top flap. Then glue the matching picture underneath.
5. After the children read the word on the front, they can "look and see" if their answer is correct.

Adaptation:
* Make "look and see" games to help children with name identification, sets, math facts, initial consonant sounds, and other skills.

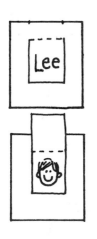

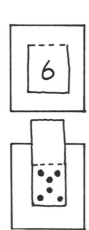

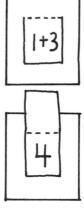

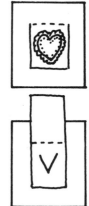

WORD HUNT

Skill:	sight words
Materials:	* yardstick or other pointer
	* silly hat
Directions:	1. Let the children put on the hat, go around the room, and point to words they can read.
	2. Pick one child to be "teacher," to point to words as his or her classmates read them.

Adaptations:

* Turn off the lights and let the children read words as you point to them with a flashlight.

* Walk around the school and have the children hunt for words in their environment that they can read. Make a language experience chart of these words.

* Read words along the road when you go on a field trip.

* Ask the children to go on a word hunt around their homes to find all the words they can read. (This might be a fun activity for children to do with their parents.)

* Make a list of common words in your classroom and attach the list to a clipboard. Give the children a pencil and let them go around the room and hunt for those words. As they find each word they can cross it off the list. (Two children may enjoy working on this together.)

* Go on a number hunt and make a list of how numerals are used in the school.

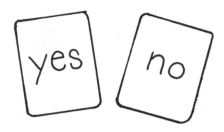

YES—NO CARDS

Skill:	listening and recall

Materials:
* ✱ 3" × 5" index cards or cardboard cut to that size
* ✱ red and green markers
* ✱ paper clip

Directions:

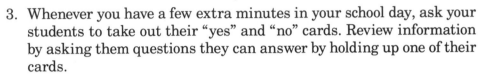

1. Print "yes" on one card with the green marker, and print "no" on the other card with the red marker. Paper clip the two cards together.
2. Make one set for each child in your room.
3. Whenever you have a few extra minutes in your school day, ask your students to take out their "yes" and "no" cards. Review information by asking them questions they can answer by holding up one of their cards.

Adaptation:

✱ These cards can be used for almost any subject or content. For example:

—If you want to reinforce safety skills, you might say:

"You should always wear your seat belt."

"You can ride with strangers."

—To review letter sounds, you might say:

"Telephone begins with the letter *F*."

"Cake has the long *U* sound."

—For science or social studies, you might say:

"Spiders have eight legs."

"Texas is our state."

Note: These cards involve each child and encourage good listening skills.

WRITER'S WORKSHOP

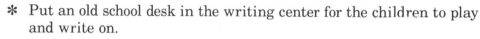

Skill: creative writing

Materials:
* ✱ table and chairs
* ✱ pens, pencils, markers, crayons
* ✱ chalkboard and chalk, magic slate
* ✱ scissors, tape, stickers, stamps
* ✱ variety of paper, envelopes, self-stick notes, sentence strips, graph paper, and so forth
* ✱ blank books
* ✱ manual typewriter

Directions:
1. Create a "writer's workshop" in a quiet corner of your classroom.
2. Encourage children to go to the "writer's workshop." Then display their work in the "writer's gallery" on the walls around it.

Adaptations:

* ✱ Put an old school desk in the writing center for the children to play and write on.
* ✱ Store writing paraphernalia in a shoe rack or similar container with compartments.
* ✱ Vary materials frequently to keep children interested.
* ✱ Set up a writing station on the playground under a tree. Put out a table and chairs, paper, markers, and other writing materials for the children to use.
* ✱ Fill a detergent box with a handle with pens, paper, envelopes, self-stick notes, blank books, and so on, for the children to check out and take home.
* ✱ Print shops are usually glad to give you scrap paper, or parents who work in offices may be able to bring you old envelopes, used computer paper, or junk mail.

 **MAILBOXES**

Skill: writing

Materials:
* 8" × 5" or 9" × 12" clasp envelopes
* crayons or markers
* red construction paper
* brad fasteners
* scissors
* paper, envelopes, pens, pencils

Directions:
1. Give children clasp envelopes and let them decorate them with their name and picture to make a mailbox.
2. Cut flags from red construction paper and attach to the envelopes with a brad fastener.
3. Tape the mailboxes to cubbies or desks, or staple to a bulletin board.
4. Children can write notes and letters and deliver them to each others' mailboxes.

Adaptations:

* Set up a mail system within your school for children to send letters to friends in other classrooms.
* Make a mailbox for your own desk from a shoebox or cereal box. Tell the children if they have something personal they want you to know about, they can write it and put it in your box. This can also be used for suggestions or complaints!
* Give children junk mail to open and write on.

© 1994 by The Center for Applied Research in Education

46

ACTION ILLUSTRATIONS

Skill: prewriting

Materials:
* chalkboard or large chart paper
* marker or chalk
* paper and crayons for children

Directions:
1. Ask the children to look out the window and tell you some objects they see moving outside, such as the wind. "The wind blows like this." (Make big slanting movements in front of your body.) Ask the children to imitate your actions.
2. Draw slanting strokes on the board, while the children make a row of slanting lines across their paper.
3. Continue with different movements that allow the children to practice various strokes. For example:

The wind blows.	\ \ \ \ \ \ \ \ \ \
Squirrels run around.	llllll
The rain falls.	: : : : : : : : :
Bunnies hop.	⌒⌒⌒⌒⌒⌒
Cars zoom.	————
Birds fly.	∿∿∿∿

Note: This is a positive way to exercise small muscles while giving children success.

Adaptations:
* Cut old file folders in two. Draw straight lines, curves, shapes, and so forth, on the cards with markers. Laminate or cover with self-stick vinyl. Give the children play dough or clay and let them reproduce the shapes on top of the cards.
* Give children yarn pieces or beans to lay on top of different shapes.

 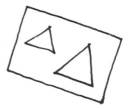

READING POOL

Skill:	reading
Materials:	* plastic swimming pool
	* pillows
	* books and magazines
	* stuffed animals (book buddies)

Directions:

1. Fill the pool with old pillows, books, and magazines.
2. Allow children to sit in the pool and read.
3. Add stuffed animals (book buddies) for the children to read to.

Adaptations:

* A reading tent can also entice readers. Make a tent by putting a blanket over a table. Add a sleeping bag, flashlight, and books for the children to read. (This would also be a great idea for the playground.)

* A reading loft or wooden platform offers another special place for children to look at books.

* Older children might enjoy a reader's corner. Place a small table, lamp, books, magazines, rocking chair, beanbag chairs, and so on, in a corner of the classroom. When the children want to read, they can turn on the lamp and get "cozy" with a book.

* Building a reader's doghouse would be a fun activity for the whole class. Get an old appliance box and let the children paint it to look like a doghouse. Fill it with pillows and books and let the reading begin! (You might even add some stuffed toy dogs.)

 **WALK A STORY**

 Title

Author

Illustrator

Skill: elements of a story

Materials:
* cardboard or heavy paper
* scissors
* markers
* tape

Directions:
1. Cut out the shapes below from cardboard and write the parts of a story on them as shown.

 Characters

 Setting

 Problem

Beginning

Middle

 End (Solution)

2. Place these on the floor with tape.
3. After reading a book, children can take turns standing on the shapes and identifying those things from the story.

Note: If you begin discussing authors, illustrators, and the above elements in books when the children are young, it will improve their ability to answer comprehension questions as they grow older.

 **STORY BOARD**

Skill: oral language

Materials:
* bulletin board
* felt cut the size of the bulletin board
* stapler, scissors
* colorful fabric or juvenile print (three yards)
* flannel board story pieces

Directions:
1. Cover the area of the bulletin board you want to use with felt and staple in place.
2. Cut the fabric in half. Staple it to the top of the board, then drape it down the sides to resemble stage curtains as shown.
3. Let the children take turns retelling stories with the felt pieces.

Adaptations:
* Use an old sheet for the curtain.
* Cover the back of a bookshelf or divider with felt to make a similar story board.
* Choose one child each day to be the "storyteller of the day."
* To make felt pieces stick better, attach a little Velcro™ (loop side) to the back of each piece.
* Use the story board for math activities.
* A flannel board that is light and easy to use can be made from a fabric bolt. Cover the bolt with felt, then attach a piece of ribbon to one end of the board. Hang it around your neck so your hands will be free to tell the story.

TREASURE HUNT STORY

Skill: love of books; following directions

Materials:
* book
* clues written on paper

Directions:

1. Before play time, place four to five clues on the playground that will lead to the "treasure story." For example:

    "A treasure hunt is so much fun. In the sandbox is Clue #1."

    "Clue #2 should be easy, too. At the top of the slide is something for you."

    "Clue #3 you will see up in a tree."

    "Clue #4 is near the door."

    "Our treasure hunt is almost through, and the prize is a special book for you. In the bushes is where you should look to find a wonderful book."

2. Read the clues and let the children follow directions to find subsequent clues.

3. Have story time on the playground when the children find the book.

Adaptations:

* Hide a stuffed animal with the book for the children to find.
* Let the children draw their own treasure maps.
* Adapt the treasure hunt for a holiday and hide treats in a pumpkin or Easter basket.

CAMPFIRE STORIES

Skill:	oral language
Materials:	* rocks and sticks
Directions:	1. Encourage the children to help you build a campfire for your playground by collecting rocks and sticks. (Instead of throwing rocks and sticks, you can use them for your campfire.)
	2. Sit around the campfire and let the children make up stories or sing songs.
Adaptations:	* Ask open-ended questions for children to complete, such as:

> I wish I were a cloud because . . . .
> If I were a tree I would . . . .
> I wish I were a (animal) because . . . .
> One thing I would do to clean up the earth is . . . .

* If you have a large rock on your playground and you don't know what to do with it, then make it your wishing rock. Read *Sylvester and the Magic Pebble* to the children. Then let each of them stand on the rock and make a wish.

STORY CAN

Skill: oral language

Materials:
* construction paper (yellow, red, green, and blue)
* scissors, markers, tape
* potato chip canister or other tall can

Directions:
1. Decorate the can with construction paper.
2. Cut the construction paper into 2½" × 9" strips. You will need five of each color.
3. Print the following on the strips:

red —	Who?	Good Fairy
	Who?	Mean Giant
	Who?	Superman
	Who?	Little Old Lady
	Who?	Big Bad Wolf
blue —	When?	Long ago
	When?	Last week
	When?	Tomorrow
	When?	Right now
	When?	At midnight
green —	Where?	Woods
	Where?	Outer space
	Where?	Jungle
	Where?	School
	Where?	Magic kingdom
yellow —	What?	Granted a magic wish
	What?	Fell in a hole
	What?	Found a treasure map
	What?	Disappeared
	What?	Saved the day

4. Children select a strip of each color from the can, then make up a story using those elements. Younger children can tell a story or draw a picture, while older children can write their own story.

HOMEMADE BOOKS

Children love to make books, which are a perfect way to reinforce reading and writing skills.

Baggie Book:

Cut construction paper to fit inside a plastic bag. Draw a picture, or glue on a photograph or magazine picture. Insert the picture in the baggie and zip it up. Put several of these together with a book ring, pipe cleaner, or ribbon to make a book.

Lunch Bag Book:

Take four or five lunch bags and fold the bottom over to one side. Glue an animal shape or other picture so part of it is hidden under the flap. Put the pages of the book together with a brad fastener or yarn. Children can try to guess what the animal is, then open the flap to see if they are correct. Older children can write riddles or other questions on the bag, then hide the answer under the flap.

Class Books:

Let everyone in the class draw a picture and write or dictate a sentence to go with it. Put the pages together and make a book the whole class can enjoy. Some topics might be:

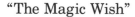

"The Magic Wish"
"I Would Like to Tell the President"
"If I Were in Charge of the World"
"My Nightmare Looks Like"
"Things to Be Happy About"
"My Invention"
"I Can Do Something Special"
"When I Get Mad"
"How to Save Our Planet Earth"
"When I Grow Up"
"If I Won a Million Dollars"

Let the children take turns checking these books out to take home and share with their families.

Teeny Tiny Book:

Sometimes children like big books, and sometimes they like little tiny books. Cut paper into 3" × 2" rectangles and staple together for creative book making.

Tag-Along Book:

Attach a pipe cleaner handle to a homemade book and it will "tag along" with you wherever you go.

Step Book:

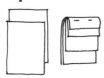

Take two sheets of paper and layer them about 2" apart as shown. Fold backwards, then staple at the top to make four pages. This is a good book for writing a story in sequence. (Add more pages according to the ability of your students.)

Big Book Joke Book:

Cut large sheets of posterboard in half. Divide children into pairs, and give each pair a piece of this posterboard. On the front they write a riddle, and on the back they draw the answer. Put all the pages together with book rings to make a class big book.

Grocery Bag Big Book:

Cut the front and back off grocery bags. Let the children draw pictures or write stories on these, then put them together with yarn to make a book. This is a fun book for illustrating songs or poems, such as "Frog Went a-Courtin'," "Old MacDonald's Farm," or "Five Little Monkeys."

Shape Books:

Cut construction paper and inside pages in various shapes to correlate with a unit of study, book, concept, and so forth.

Wallpaper Book:

Cover cardboard with wallpaper scraps to make the outside of a book. Staple blank sheets of paper inside.

Cereal Box Book:

Cut off the front and back of a cereal or other food box. Cut paper to fit inside. Punch holes and tie with yarn.

Fabric Book:

Glue fabric scraps to cardboard to make the outside cover for a book.

Self-Stick Vinyl:

Attach self-stick vinyl to the front and back cover of a homemade book.

Mylar Balloon:

Cut apart an old mylar balloon. Laminate it, then cut newsprint pages to fit inside. Use ribbon, a brad fastener, or book ring to put it together.

FUN WAYS TO EXTEND A BOOK

What can you do after you've finished reading a book? Don't put it back on the shelf! Integrate literature with art, science, cooking, math, and every area of your curriculum with one of these ideas.

Art:

Mural: Let the children paint or color a large mural illustrating the story.

Clay: Give clay to the children and ask them to make a character from the story.

Puppet: Make a bag, stick, sock, finger, or coat hanger puppet of a favorite character.

Book Jacket: Create a book jacket representing the story.

Bookmark: Make a bookmark to use as you read the book.

Pop-up Picture: Illustrate a favorite scene from the book using the directions for "Pop-ups" activity.

Poster: Let two children design a poster about the book.

Windsock: Decorate a windsock to go along with a book.

Diorama: Make a diorama from a shoebox about the book.

Pennant: Design a pennant of a favorite book.

Cartoon: Make a cartoon about a favorite scene in the book.

Mobile: Cut out characters from a story and hang them from a paper plate rim or hanger to make a mobile.

Collage: Cut up old magazines and newspapers to make a collage that represents a story.

Big Book: Let several children work together to make a big book version for the class.

Shape Book: Choose a shape that represents a story and make a book.

T-Shirt: Design a t-shirt of a favorite book.

Mask: Make a paper plate mask of a story character.

Costume: Create a costume from a brown grocery bag, newspaper, yarn, old clothes, and so on.

Hat: Decorate a hat like a favorite book.

Paint: Paint a picture.

Bumper Sticker: Design a bumper sticker about a book.

Class Quilt: Let every child draw a picture of his or her favorite book on a piece of fabric. Sew them together to make a class quilt.

Paper Dolls: Cut out paper dolls, then decorate them like characters in a book.

Music:

Rap: Make up a rap, song, or finger play that relates to a book.

Dance: Make up a dance about a story.

Background Music: Play background music to accompany a story.

Instruments: Use musical instruments to tell a story. (For example, a drum could represent a wolf; bells, the fairy; wood blocks, a horse; and so forth.)

New Words: Make up original words to a familiar tune.

Tape or Video: Record dramatizations of stories when the class performs them.

Cooking:

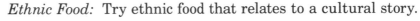

Book Cooks: Cook something that relates to a story read, such as gingerbread kids, pigs in a blanket, or blueberry muffins.

Cookbooks: Make cookbooks of favorite recipes for children to take home at the end of the year.

Sequence Cards: Let children follow directions on sequence cards to make their own snacks.

Ethnic Food: Try ethnic food that relates to a cultural story.

Dictation: Let children dictate recipes to you, then put them together to make a cookbook.

Social Studies:

Time Line: Make a time line about a story.

Map: Draw a story map that illustrates a story.

Globe: Point out on a map or globe where a story takes place.

Culture: Discuss the culture depicted in a book. How is it like their culture? How is it different?

Antibias: Read stories depicting men and women of all ages, abilities, and ethnic groups in positive roles.

Author's Background: Share the author's cultural background with the children.

Math:

Graphs: Make a graph comparing favorite books, characters, and authors.

Word Problems: Make up number stories from different elements in a story.

Classification: Classify books that are real or pretend, funny or sad, long or short, and other attributes.

Time: Discuss the amount of time that lapses in a story.

Measurement: Talk about distances traveled in a story.

Science:

Animals: Discuss characteristics of different animals depicted in stories.

Changes: Point out seasons, growth, and changes that occur in a story.

Experiment: Do an experiment that relates to a story.

Predict: Let children make predictions about what might happen in a story.

Field Trips: Take a field trip that relates to a story.

Research: Do research about a character or event in a story that children want to know more about.

Social/Emotional:

Bibliotherapy: Read stories with characters who have similar problems to children in your classroom. These can offer children alternative behaviors and be a source of healing.

Models: Provide children with stories about heros that can give them courage.

Values Clarification: Tell stories that will help children with moral issues and decisions they will face.

Role Playing: Let children act out book characters with different points of view. Discuss how they would solve a problem.

Projects: Give children cooperative learning projects where they can learn to work together.

Speaking:

Storytelling: Encourage children to tell stories orally to classmates.

Book Talks: Let children sit around informally and discuss books they have read.

Interview: Ask children to interview a classmate, parent, or friend about books they like to read.

Dramatizations: Children love to perform, so let them act out a story.

Sound Effects: Children will enjoy making sound effects (wind, siren, rain, crying) as you read a book.

Dress-Up: Ask children to dress like a favorite character in a story and tell the story from his or her point of view.

Circle Story: Have the children sit in a circle. You begin a story, then each child adds a sentence or more to it as you go around the circle.

Recording Studio: Set up a large box with a tape recorder in a quiet area of the room where the children can go and tell stories or read into the recorder.

Puppets: Let the children tell stories using puppets or flannel board pieces.

Listening:

Guest Reader: Invite a parent, principal, grandparent, sibling, politician, athlete, or other special person to come read to your class.

Leave Out a Word: As you read a story, leave out a word and see who can fill it in.

Listening Center: Provide children with stories to listen to, or let them make their own storytelling tapes for your Listening Center.

Poetry Break: Take a break during your busy day and read poetry to your class.

Riddles: Make up riddles about characters or events in a story.

Writing:

Homemade Books: Let the children make homemade books about a story.

Language Experience: Make a language experience chart recalling the events of a story.

Ending: Have the children write a new ending to a story.

Letter: Write a letter to a favorite character in a story, or write a letter to the author.

TV Commercial: Ask the children to write a TV commercial advertising a book.

Poem: Write a poem about a story.

Play: Let the children work in pairs to write a play about a story.

Newspaper Article: Ask the children to write a review of a book or to write a feature story based on some event.

Journal: Give children an opportunity to respond to stories read in a journal.

Writing Center: Create a special place where children can write and explore with different writing materials.

Edit: Encourage children to edit and rewrite their work. (Two children might enjoy doing this together.)

Comic Strip: Let children tell a story using cartoon characters with bubbles coming out of their mouths.

Spelling:

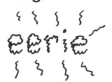

Word of the Day: Use a new word from a story as "word of the day." Look it up in the dictionary and talk about what it means.

Personal Dictionary: Let the children make a word file of new words they learn. They can use these in writing their own stories.

Rainbow Words: To learn new words, have the children trace around them with several different colors of crayons to make them look like a rainbow.

Glue Words: Write words with glue on cardboard, then children can feel them or do rubbings of them.

Puzzle: Make a crossword puzzle or wordsearch of new vocabulary words from a story.

Alphabetical Order: Put vocabulary words in alphabetical order.

Reading:

Choral Reading: Read a section of a book out loud together.

Author Study: Go to the library and find out about a favorite author.

Shadow Reading: Let one child read a line, then another child read the same line. (This is an effective way to pair a capable student with one who needs help.)

Read It Again: Encourage children to reread stories. (They will enjoy having you read favorite stories again, too.)

Reading Portfolio: Have the children keep a list of all the books they read during the year.

Book Party: Plan a classroom party for a favorite book character.

Book Bucks: Let the children make a paper billfold and paper dollars. When they hear about a good book they would like to read, have them write the title and author on one of their "book bucks." When they go to the library to check out a book, they can take their book bucks with them.

Games: Make games based on the setting, sequence, characters, and other elements of a story.

'TIS THE SEASON

Adapt language games to holidays, seasons, or teaching themes.

 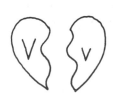

Match upper- and lower-case letters on valentines.

Match colored flowers to the correct word on the flower pot.

Discriminate like jelly beans.

Rhyme pictures on eggs.

Put pictures in pails with initial consonant sounds.

Word family games.

Pop-up games of seasonal words.

Homemade books.

I am thankful
   for....
Jan: my house
Chad: my dog
Rosie: good food

Language experience stories.

Sight words.

60

© 1994 by The Center for Applied Research in Education

Math Magic Activities

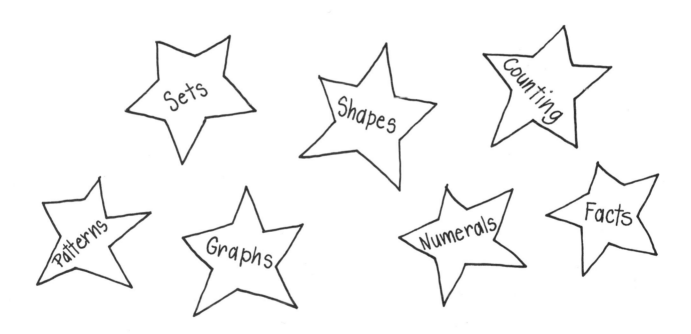

"Math lovers" are what you'll have with the hands-on activities in this section. Coupons, sticks, cereal boxes, pasta, telephone, dishes, and more become the tools for developing math concepts while playing and having fun.

SET THE TABLE

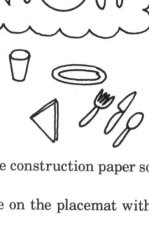

Skill: one-to-one correspondence

Materials:
*   construction paper
*   plastic forks, spoons, knives
*   paper cups, plates, napkins
*   scissors, markers

Directions:
1. Cut a scalloped edge on the outer edges of the construction paper so it looks like a placemat.
2. Trace the cup, plate, napkin, and silverware on the placemat with markers.
3. Ask the children to match items with the outlines on placemats.

Adaptations:

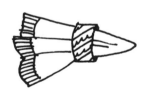

*   Give children different amounts of cups, plates, and silverware. As they try to set a table, ask them if they have enough of everything. "What do you need more of? How many more do you need?"
*   Put this activity in the Housekeeping Center for children to play with.
*   Encourage children to set the table for snacks and meals in your classroom.
*   Let the children pass out books, crayons, and other objects.
*   Collect different sizes of cups, plates, and silverware, and ask the children to seriate them by size to set the table.
*   Make napkin rings from toilet paper rolls by cutting them into 1" strips. Decorate with markers, then ask the children to match paper napkins in them using one-to-one correspondence.
*   Let children match muffin papers in a muffin pan or put tennis balls in a muffin pan. Children can also put plastic eggs in an egg carton to practice one-to-one matching.

BUBBLE GUM

Skill: one-to-one correspondence

Materials:
* posterboard
* construction paper
* scissors, glue
* aluminum foil
* pennies

Directions:

1. Cut out several bubble gum machines from posterboard using the patterns on the following page. Cover with aluminum foil.
2. Cut out "bubble gum" of different colors from construction paper.
3. Glue different amounts of bubble gum to the machines.
4. Give children pennies and ask them to match pennies one-to-one with the bubble gum.
5. Count the number of pieces of bubble gum and pennies in each machine.

Adaptations:

* Match numeral cards with the number of pieces of bubble gum in each machine.
* Use bubble gum machines to make matching games for colors, upper- and lower-case letters, math facts, and so forth.

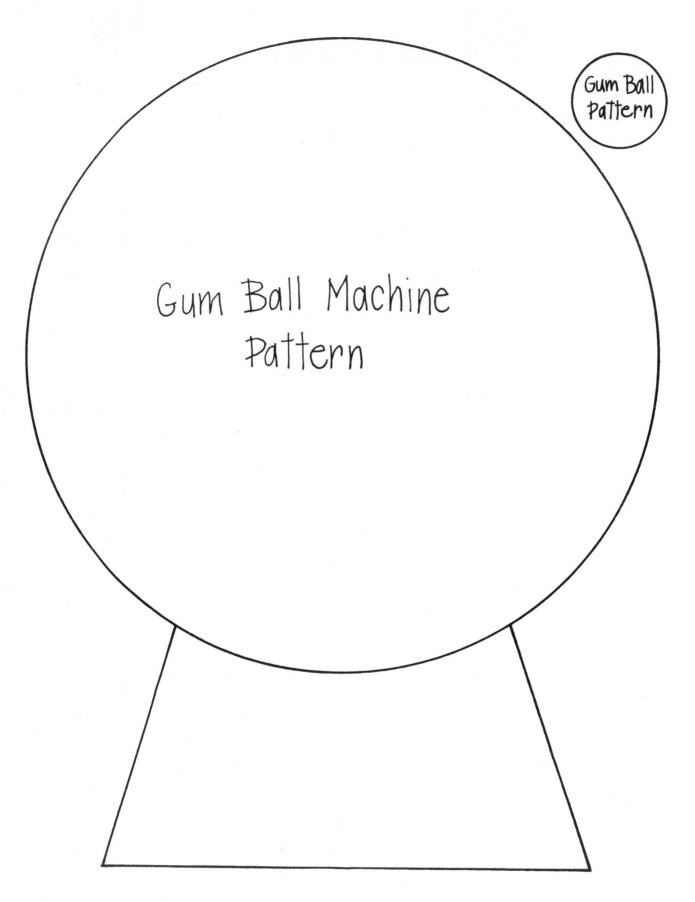

Gum Ball Machine
Pattern

Gum Ball
Pattern

FEED THE BUNNIES

Skill: one-to-one correspondence

Materials:
* construction paper (brown, orange, green)
* scissors, glue, markers
* storage bag or envelope

Directions:
1. Cut out eight brown bunnies.
2. Cut out eight orange carrots. Cut stems out of green paper and glue to carrots.
3. Place three bunnies in front of the child and hand him or her three carrots. Ask the child to feed each bunny a carrot. "Do you have the same amount of bunnies as carrots? How can you tell?"
4. Continue giving the child different sets of bunnies and carrots to feed them.
5. Store pieces in the plastic bag or envelope.

Adaptation:
* This game can be used to reinforce sets and numerals, upper- and lower-case letters, math facts, and so forth.

PASTA! PASTA!

Skill: patterns

Materials:
* shaped pasta (shells, bears, or other interesting shapes)
* food coloring
* rubbing alcohol
* 4 plastic bags
* wax paper

Directions:
1. Divide pasta into fourths and put each fourth in a plastic bag.
2. Add one tablespoon of rubbing alcohol and approximately ten drops of food coloring to each bag.
3. Shake until all pasta is evenly colored.
4. Spread in a single layer on wax paper to dry.
5. Make a simple pattern from the pasta. Then ask the children to extend it.
6. Let the children make up their own patterns with the pasta.

Adaptations:
* Take 3" × 6" pieces of cardboard and glue a different pattern to each card that the children can reproduce.

* Use the pasta for sorting activities, asking the children to sort it in muffin pans, berry baskets, or egg cartons.
* Have the children make sets and do addition and subtraction problems with the pasta.

NATURE PATTERNS

Skill: patterns

Materials:
* leaves, sticks, rocks, and other natural objects

Directions:
1. Begin with two different kinds of objects.
2. Place a leaf, then a rock, a leaf, then a rock, leaf, rock. "What would come next?"
3. Let the children reproduce the pattern.
4. Have the children make up their own patterns with objects from nature.

Adaptations:

* Make up patterns with the children. Have one child hold his or her arms up, the next child keeps arms down, and so on. Ask the children to think of other patterns they could make with their bodies.
* Encourage children to make a pattern when stringing wooden beads or doing an art project, such as vegetable printing.
* Let two children play a pattern game. One child makes a pattern, then the other child tries to extend it.
* Use ordinary classroom objects, such as blocks, crayons, or toy dishes, to make patterns.
* Look for patterns in nature and the world around us, such as seasons, plant life, and so forth.

"HAVE IT YOUR WAY" HAMBURGERS

Skill: sorting

Materials:
* felt (black, brown, yellow, red, green)
* scissors
* container with dividers or plastic bags

Directions:
1. Cut out several hamburger buns, hamburgers, tomatoes, lettuce, pickles, and cheese slices from the felt using the patterns on the following page.
2. Separate the different felt pieces into a divided container, or use plastic bags.
3. Give the children the pieces and let them pretend to make hamburgers.
4. When they are finished playing, ask the children to sort the different ingredients and put them back where they belong.

Adaptations:

* After a child makes a hamburger, ask him or her to count the number of ingredients he or she put on it.
* Have the children make three hamburgers with everything on them. This will give them experience in matching objects one-to-one.
* Ask the children to make a pattern with the felt pieces.
* Let the children make a hamburger collage from construction paper cut in similar shapes.
* You can make other sorting games by making tacos (shells, meat, cheese, lettuce, tomatoes) or sub sandwiches (bread, meat, cheese, lettuce, onions) from felt or construction paper.

Bun
Pattern

(Brown)

Hamburger
Pattern

(Black)

Lettuce
Pattern

(Green)

Cheese
Pattern

(Yellow)

Pickle
Pattern
(Green)

Tomato
Pattern

(Red)

THE SET MONSTER

Skill: sets

Materials:
* lunch bag
* crayons or markers
* glue, scissors

Directions:

1. Color and cut out the "Set Monster" on the following page and glue it to a lunch bag to make a puppet.

2. Introduce the "Set Monster" to the children: "This is my friend, the Set Monster. He's always hungry and loves to eat things, but he can only eat sets of objects." Ask the children to help you find some sets in the room that the Set Monster could eat. For example, a set of books, blocks, chairs, cars—even a set of children!

3. Let one child at a time take the puppet and pretend to eat a set in the classroom. Ask, "Why is it a set?" "How are the things alike?"

Adaptations:

* Allow each child to make his or her own paper bag Set Monster.

* Take a walk around the school or playground and identify different sets for the Set Monster to eat.

* Give children a box with three or four of several different items, such as coins, pencils, or blocks. Ask them to make sets of like objects.

* Let the children make sets by sorting party mix or cereal of different shapes.

* Have the children sort plastic silverware into like sets in a tray.

* Dismiss children from Circle Time by sets. "The set of children wearing blue may go to a center. The set of children wearing green may go to a center."

* Encourage the children to count the objects in sets.

Monster Head Pattern

Monster Mouth Pattern

SET MONSTER PATTERN

Glue the head to the bottom of a lunch bag, then glue the mouth under the flap so it will look like the monster is eating.

SORT OF

Skill: sorting; classifying

Materials: * sacks, baskets, or pails

Directions:

1. Ask the children to collect different items on the playground. (This will vary with the season and your environment.) It might be leaves, rocks, nuts, and so on.

2. Put them together in a big pile. "How can we group these?" "Can you put the things that are alike together?"

3. After the children have sorted objects, ask "How are these things alike?" "How are they different from the other groups?"

Adaptations:

* Let the children count the objects in each set or group.

* Make a graph to compare the different groups.

* Older children may be able to "regroup" objects by another attribute. "Can you think of another way you could sort these objects?"

* Give children coins, buttons, snack mix, toys, clothes, and other common objects to sort. Challenge older children to regroup objects a second or third time.

* Use a relish tray for sorting activities.

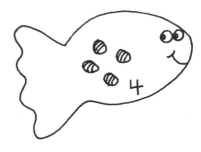

MATH MATS

Skill: sorting; sets

Materials:
* construction paper or posterboard
* scissors, markers, crayons
* packaging "peanuts" (styrofoam), seashells, seeds, nuts, pasta, pebbles, and other plentiful objects
* self-locking plastic bags

Directions:

1. Make each child a math mat in the shape of an elephant, fish, squirrel, pumpkin, dinosaur, and so forth. Make the mats to correspond with a season, unit of study, or an animal or object the children like. The mats can be made from construction paper or posterboard and should measure approximately 16" × 10".
2. Let the children decorate their mat with crayons or markers.
3. Give each child a plastic bag with counters they can use on their math mat. For example, styrofoam peanuts could be used with elephants, shells could be used with fish, seeds could be used with pumpkins, and pebbles could be used with dinosaurs.
4. Allow the children to explore freely with their counters on their mats. Then use the mats to practice making sets, sorting objects, reproducing a pattern, telling number stories, joining and separating sets, and so on.

Adaptation:

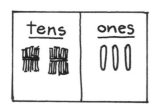

* Make a "tens and ones" mat when doing place value. Divide a rectangular sheet of paper in half. On the left write "tens" and on the right write "ones." Have the children bundle sets of tens with craft sticks, straws, and toothpicks. Ask them to make different combinations of numerals, tell you how many tens and ones, and so on.

CEREAL BOX GAME

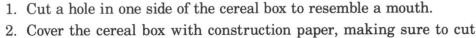

Skill: sorting; sets

Materials:
* empty cereal box
* construction paper
* scissors, markers, glue
* toothpicks

Directions:

1. Cut a hole in one side of the cereal box to resemble a mouth.
2. Cover the cereal box with construction paper, making sure to cut out where the mouth is. Add features to make face, hair, and so forth.
3. Make lollipops by gluing 1½" circles of different colors of construction paper to the ends of the toothpicks.
4. Tell children that "Lulu" is very hungry and would like to eat a set of red lollipops. Let one child sort out all the red lollipops and put them in Lulu's mouth.
5. Continue asking the children to sort out different sets of lollipops to feed Lulu. You could also ask them to feed her different amounts, such as "four lollipops" or "seven lollipops."

Adaptations:

* Have an assortment of pictures of objects beginning with different sounds. (Magazines and catalogs are a good source for these pictures.) Ask the children to feed Lulu all the things that start with "s," and so forth.
* Make a lion, bear, or other animal from a cereal box. Have the children sort out sets, make up number stories, select objects beginning with a particular sound, and so on.

© 1994 by The Center for Applied Research in Education

DECKS OF FUN

Skill: sorting

Materials:
* deck of cards

Directions:
1. Shuffle the cards.
2. Have the children sort cards by suit.

Adaptations:
* Sort cards by value.
* Put a suit of cards in numerical order. (You may want to take out the face cards before you ask the children to do this.)
* Play "Go Fish" where children are to identify different values on cards and ask other players for them.
* Play "War" where children turn over one card at a time, and the child with the largest number wins.
* Deal a story with the cards. Deal each child a card and ask him or her to make up a sentence using the numeral on the card.
* Have the children create patterns of black and red with the cards.
* Let the children stack the cards to make card houses.
* Play "52 Pick Up"! Hide the cards around the room, then let the children find them.
* Using two suits of cards, play a concentration game. A pair would be two cards of like value.
* Deal each child a card and tell him or her to keep it a secret. One at a time, let the children clap out the numeral on their card while classmates try to guess what it is.
* Get two decks of cards and ask the children to match up like cards from each deck.

PANCAKE FLIP

Skill: sets

Materials:
* yellow posterboard
* black posterboard
* spatula
* markers
* *optional:* brad or stapler

Directions:

1. Cut five to ten yellow 4" circles from the posterboard. On each circle draw a different set of spots. On the back of the circle print the numeral for the set on the front. These are your pancakes.

2. Cut a 12" circle from the black posterboard. This will be your skillet. You can also cut a handle for the skillet that is 2" × 9" and attach it with a brad or stapler.

3. Children place the pancakes on the skillet, count the spots on the front, then "flip" it over with the spatula to check their answer on the back.

Adaptation:

* Use this game for math facts, contractions, word recognition, and so on.

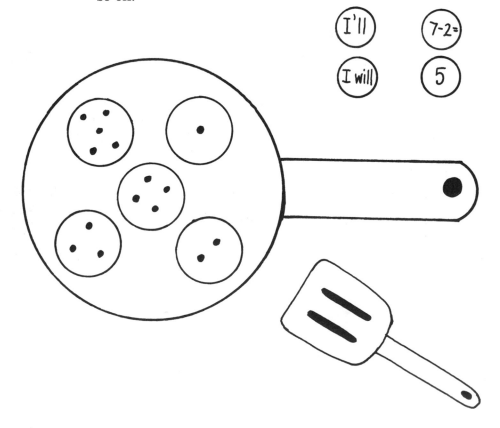

BLUEBERRY BUCKETS

Skill: sets and numerals

Materials:
* dried lima beans
* blue spray paint
* nut cups
* pipe cleaners

Directions:

1. Spread dried beans on a newspaper outside and spray with blue paint. Allow to dry, then turn them over and spray the other side. (CAUTION: Keep the children away from the spray paint's fumes.)
2. Write numerals from 0 to 10 on the sides of the nut cups. Cut a pipe cleaner in half, then attach to the nut cup to make a handle.
3. Ask the children to make sets of blueberries (beans) in the buckets.

Adaptations:

* This is a great math activity after reading *Blueberries for Sal* by Robert McCloskey. (Eat fresh blueberries or make blueberry muffins for extra fun.)
* Print math facts or number words on the sides of the cups and use the blueberries (beans) to make sets.
* Let the children estimate the number of beans in various containers.
* Let the children sort mixed dried beans in buckets.
* Spray beans other colors to go along with different themes and holidays. Use red to make apples, orange to make pumpkins, or pastel colors for Easter eggs.

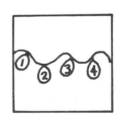

FRENCH FRIES

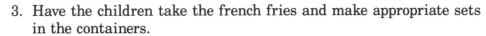

Skill: sets and numerals

Materials:
* 2 yellow sponges
* empty fast-food french fry containers
* scissors
* markers

Directions:

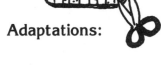

1. Cut sponges into strips to resemble french fries.
2. Print numerals on the french fry containers.
3. Have the children take the french fries and make appropriate sets in the containers.

Adaptations:

* Take several different colors of sponges and cut them into strips. Mix them up, then ask the children to sort them by colors into containers.
* Print addition facts on the containers and let the children join sets with the french fries.
* Use a similar game to reinforce place value. On one container write "hundreds," on another "tens," and on another "ones." Put some fries in each container, then ask the children to tell you the number it represents.

POT OF GOLD

Skill: sets and numerals

Materials:
* dried lima beans
* gold spray paint
* small paper cups
* construction paper, scissors, stapler

Directions:

1. Spread out lima beans on a sheet of newspaper and spray with gold paint. Allow to dry 10–15 minutes, then turn the beans over and spray the other side. (CAUTION: Keep children away from the spray paint's fumes.)

2. Cut out the pot pattern below from construction paper and print a numeral from 0 to 5 on each pot. Staple a pot to each cup.

3. Have the children count out the appropriate number of gold coins (beans) for each pot.

Adaptations:
* For older children use more cups and write larger numerals on them.
* Write math problems on the pots.
* Make up number stories using the gold coins. "I had seven coins, but I gave three to the leprechaun. How many do I have left?"
* You can also spray small rocks or gravel to be golden nuggets. Put them in a jar and let the children estimate how many there are.
* Hide the beans on the playground and let the children hunt for them. Graph results and compare amounts.

Pot
Pattern

HOORAY FOR PIZZA!

Skill: sets and numerals

Materials:
* cardboard from a pizza (or cut a 15" circle)
* spring clothespins
* markers, crayons, scissors
* construction paper

Directions:

1. Color the background of the cardboard "pizza" with red and yellow crayons to resemble tomato sauce and cheese. Use a brown marker or crayon to make the crust.
2. Divide the pizza into eight slices with a black marker.
3. Cut 36 red pepperoni slices from the construction paper.
4. Glue different amounts of pepperoni on each slice.
5. Print numerals to match the different sets on the clothespins.
6. Children count the number of pieces of pepperoni on each slice, then clip the clothespin with the appropriate numeral to it.

Adaptations:
* Make each section of the pizza wheel a different color, then print color words on the clothespins for the children to match.
* Print number words on the clothespins to match with sets.
* Match clothespins with letters on them to pictures of objects beginning with the sound on the pizza wheel.

© 1994 by The Center for Applied Research in Education

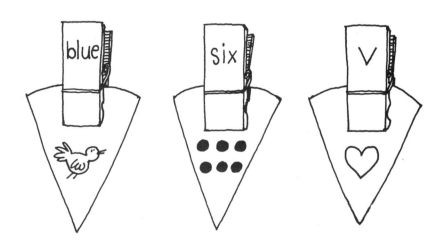

CRAFT STICK PEOPLE

Skill: sets and numerals

Materials:
* jumbo craft sticks
* fine-tip markers
* glue gun or school glue
* yarn
* scissors
* milk cartons
* construction paper

Directions:

1. Take 10–20 craft sticks and draw a different face on each stick with the felt-tip pens. Glue yarn for hair.
2. Clean and wash milk cartons. Cut off the tops, then cover with construction paper. Decorate the cartons with two windows and a door to resemble houses. Print numerals from 1 to 5 on each door.
3. The children should then take the stick people and make appropriate sets for each house.

Adaptations:
* Let the children make their own stick people for counting and math games.
* Use the stick people for joining and separating sets.
* Draw different facial expressions on the sticks and talk about feelings.
* Print numerals from 1 to 10 on the sticks, then ask the children to put them in numerical order.
* Print the letters of the alphabet on the sticks and have the children put them in alphabetical order.

TREES AND TRUNKS

Skill: sets and numerals

Materials:
* cardboard dowels (toilet paper rolls)
* green construction paper or green posterboard
* scissors, markers

Directions:
1. Trace around the tree pattern below from green paper.
2. Cut a 1½" slit on either side of the cardboard dowel.
3. Draw sets of fruit (apples, oranges, and so forth) on the trees and write matching numerals on the trunks.
4. Let the children match sets with numerals by slipping the tree into the slits on the trunk.

Adaptation:
* Use for matching upper- and lower-case letters, beginning sounds, or number words and numerals.

Tree Top Pattern

Note: Cardboard dowels are handy to stand up animals, story characters, paper houses, and other objects.

TENNIS BALL PALS

Skill: sets

Materials:
* old tennis balls
* yarn, buttons, wiggly eyes
* markers
* glue gun or white glue
* dried beans

Directions:

1. Cut a 2" slit between the seams on one side of the tennis ball with a knife. (CAUTION: This must only be done by an adult.) This will be the mouth.
2. Glue on yarn for hair, buttons for eyes and nose, and so on. Add mouth lines, freckles, eyebrows, and other details with markers.
3. Squeeze the ball on the sides of the slit to make the ball talk and open its mouth.
4. Ask the children to "feed" the tennis pals various sets of beans.

Adaptations:

* Cut out little pictures, then let the children feed the puppets objects beginning with certain sounds. You could call the puppet Bobby Ball and feed him things that start with "b," or Sally, and feed her objects beginning with "s."
* Let the children make their own tennis ball pals. (Cut the slit for the mouth ahead of time.) Have them make up stories, songs, or plays to do with their puppets.
* Create animals and favorite characters from books with the tennis balls.

NUMBER HUNT

Skill: sets and numerals

Materials:
* lunch bags
* markers

Directions:
1. On the outside of each bag, print a numeral with which your children are familiar.
2. Give each child or pair of children a bag and ask them to find a set and put it in the bag.
3. Let the children share their sets with their classmates. Encourage them to count the objects in each set.
4. Have the children return the objects where they found them.

Adaptations:

1 rock
2 sticks
3 leaves
4 flowers
5 nuts

* Use the objects for sorting or classifying activities, or for joining and separating sets.
* When working on place value with older children, ask them to make sets of ten in their bags, then use the bags to practice counting by tens.
* Give directions for finding sets of different items in nature on the bags, such as "one rock," "two sticks," "three leaves," and "four nuts."

NUMBER PLEASE

Skill: numeral recognition

Materials:
* play telephone
* photographs of children
* paper, markers, glue
* scissors, hole punch
* cover from the phone book "Yellow Pages"
* book rings or yarn

Directions:

1. Glue a child's photograph to each page. Write his or her home phone number at the bottom of the page. (If you don't have photographs, let them draw self-portraits and print their name.)
2. Put the pages together and cover with the "Yellow Pages" cover from the phone book.
3. Hole punch and tie together with yarn or use book rings.
4. Children can use the phone book and play telephone, pretending to call their friends.

Adaptations:

* Let the children make their own class phone books to take home by photocopying pages for each child in the room.
* Use the play telephone to encourage oral language by asking the children to call parents or grandparents to tell them what they're learning at school.

 **SHOW ME**

Skill: numeral recognition

Materials: * cardboard or scrap paper cut in 3" × 5" rectangles
                     * markers
                     * envelope or paper clip

Directions:

1. Take 11 cards and write numerals from 0 to 10 on the cards with markers, or use the numeral cards on the following page. Paper clip the cards together or store them in an envelope.
2. Make one set for each child in the group with whom you plan to use this game.
3. Have each child spread out a set of cards in front of him or her. Clap your hands a certain number of times, then ask the children to "show me" that numeral. (You can also put a certain number of items on the flannel board, draw sets on the chalkboard, and so forth.)
4. Allow the children to take turns clapping out sets or making sets with objects.
5. With this game, you can see quickly who has grasped a concept and who needs more work.

Adaptations: * In primary grades, make a set for each student or have them make their own set. You can practice addition and subtraction facts, make up number stories, and review many different math skills with the "show me" cards.
                     * Make "show me" cards with shapes, colors, letters, and other basic skills you are working on.

"Show me your rectangle."

"Show me the sound you hear at the beginning of the word *pig*."

"Show me your card that is the color of grass."

NUMERAL CARDS FOR "SHOW ME"
AND OTHER MATH GAMES

0	1	2
3	4	5
6	7	8
9	10	Math Lover

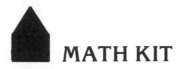 **MATH KIT**

Skill: shapes; sorting

Materials:
- * schoolbox or cigar box
- * felt, felt scraps
- * scissors, glue

Directions:
1. Cut the size of the lid from felt. Then glue it to the inside of the lid.
2. Cut small geometric shapes (circles, triangles, rectangles, squares) from the felt scraps. Store these in the box.
3. Let the children sort the shapes in the box.

Adaptations:

- * Let the children reproduce patterns with felt shapes.
- * Make additional felt objects to store in the box. Then let the children use them for joining and separating sets.
- * Make up number stories with the felt pieces.
- * Add other manipulative materials for math exploration, such as counters, objects to sort, rulers, coins, play clock, sandpaper numerals, and so forth.
- * Make story boxes by putting felt pieces for stories in similar schoolboxes.

FUNNY FACE

Skill: shape recognition

Materials:
* * construction paper or cardboard
* * markers
* * rubber cement, scissors
* * drinking glass or jar

Directions:

1. Cut the construction paper or cardboard into 8½" × 11" rectangles. Cut out the shapes below and glue them to the rectangles.

2. Trace around a glass or jar to make a small circle. Draw a silly face on the circle, or use the "funny face" below.

3. Have the children sit in a circle on the floor. In the middle of the circle lay out the shape cards, asking the children to name them with you as you lay them down.

4. Tell the children to turn around and hide their eyes. Then take "funny face" and hide it under one of the shapes.

5. Have the children turn back around and tell them to raise their hands if they think they know where "funny face" is hiding. One at a time call on a child, ask the child to name the shape he or she thinks it is under, then let the child look under that shape. Continue until a child finds "funny face." That child may then be "it" and hide "funny face."

Adaptation:

* * Children's names, animal pictures, sight words, colors, letters, numerals, and vocabulary words can all be used for this game. You can also vary the number of cards you use based on the children's age. For example, for three-year-olds you might want to use six animal pictures, but with seven-year-olds you could use 20 sight words.

Funny Face

I SPY SHAPES

Skill: shape recognition

Materials:
* construction paper or felt
* scissors
* plastic bag or envelope

Directions:
1. Cut three of each shape using the patterns on the following page. (Either construction paper or felt may be used.)
2. Mix up the shapes, then pick up a circle and say, "Does anybody see another shape that looks like this one?" Let the children find the other circles and put them together.
3. "I spy something in our room that is round like a circle. Who else sees something that looks like a circle?" Let the children take turns pointing to the circles.
4. Continue sorting the other shapes and identifying objects in the classroom that are of the same shape.

Adaptations:
* Ask the children to sort the shapes, then arrange them by size.
* Let the children put different shapes together to make objects such as ice cream cones, trees, houses, and so on. (This is fun to do with felt shapes on the flannel board.)

* Give the children paper geometric shapes for making a collage in art.
* Have a shape snack with crackers and other foods of different shapes.

"I SPY" SHAPES IN SERIATED SIZES

OUTDOOR SHAPES

Skill: shape recognition

Materials:
* cardboard cut in 6" squares
* markers

Directions:

1. Draw the following shapes on the cardboard:

2. Have the children identify shapes.
3. Show the children one shape at a time. Then let them go around the playground to see if they can match it with a similar shape. For example, the oval might match to the petal of a flower, the circle to the wheel on the tricycle, the triangle to the top of a pine tree, and so on.

Adaptations:

* Individual children or pairs of children can be given a shape card to find on the playground. Use simpler or more complex shapes depending on the ability of the children.
* Let the children draw shapes in the sandbox with their fingers, or on the sidewalk with chalk.
* Divide the children into groups of four and challenge them to make shapes with their bodies on the grass.

HAPPY BIRTHDAY TO YOU!

Skill: counting

Materials:
* heavy paper or posterboard
* markers, scissors
* birthday candles

Directions:
1. Color and cut out several birthday cakes using the pattern at the bottom of the page.
2. Put different amounts of candles on the birthday cakes.
3. Let the children take turns counting the candles on the cakes.

Adaptations:
* Give the children a birthday cake and some candles. Then ask them to put the correct number of candles on the cake for whatever age you tell them.
* Give the children play dough or clay to make "birthday cakes" to put the candles in.
* Use birthday cakes and candles for working out addition problems or recognizing number words.

Birthday cake pattern

COUNT-AT-HOME BOOK

Skill: counting

Materials:
* construction paper
* markers
* scissors, hole punch
* book rings or yarn
* laminating machine or clear self-stick vinyl
* erasable crayons or markers

Directions:
1. Cut construction paper in 8" × 6" pieces.
2. Draw pictures of items commonly found around most homes on each page. (You could also cut these out of magazines or catalogs.)

3. Decorate a cover page that says "My Count-at-Home Book."
4. Cover the pages with clear self-stick vinyl or laminate.
5. Punch holes in the pages and put together with yarn or a book ring.
6. Let one child at a time take the book home and count the various items in his or her home with his or her parents. Give children an erasable crayon or marker to write numerals with in the book.
7. Share results with classmates the following day.

Adaptation:

* Make a book for each child with blank pages titled "I Can Read." Let children cut out labels, logos, and other words they can read from magazines, the newspaper, or food cartons, and glue them in the book. (This is a great activity to help get parents involved.)

 BIG FOOT

Skill: counting

Materials:
  * heavy paper
  * scissors
  * markers
  * tape

Directions:
  1. Cut out "big feet" using the pattern on the following page.
  2. Print numerals from 0 to 10 on the feet and tape them to the floor.
  3. Let the children step on the footprints, counting aloud as they do so.

Adaptations:

  * Vary the number of footprints you make to the ability of the children in your classroom.
  * Hide "big feet" on the playground. Ask the children to find them and bring them to you in numerical order.
  * Print alphabet letters on the footprints. Place them around the room for children to step on as they sing the alphabet song.
  * For older children, write a sentence or word to a story on each footprint. Children can read the story as they move from one footprint to the next.

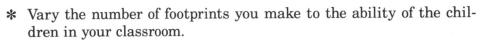
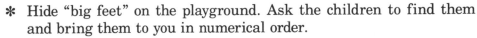

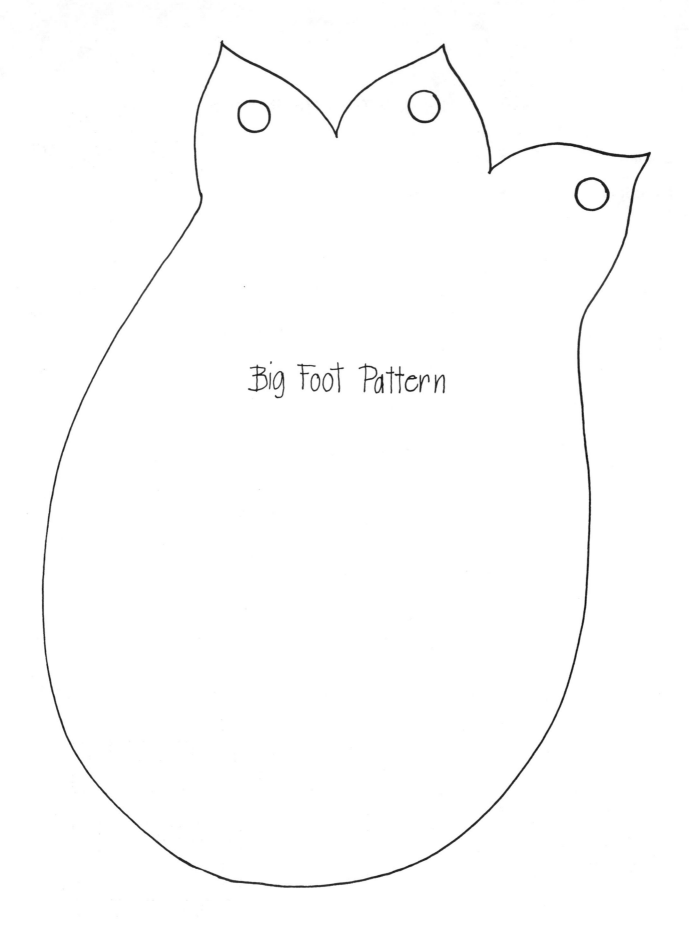

Big Foot Pattern

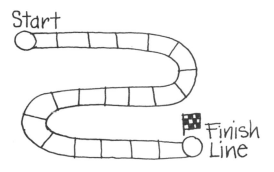

LET'S GO TO THE RACES

Skill: counting

Materials:
* cardboard
* small toy cars
* dice
* markers

Directions:

1. On the cardboard draw out a gameboard similar to the one below.
2. Children take one die, throw it, and move their car the same number of spaces. (Older children could use two dice and add the numerals.)
3. The first child to reach the finish line is the winner. Continue the game until all the children have crossed the finish line.

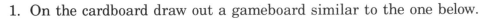

Adaptations:
* Make board games on file folders.
* Use board games to reinforce colors, letters, math facts, and other information.
* Spinners and cards can be used to tell children how many spaces to move. Bottle caps, old magic marker tops, and other small toys can be used for game pieces.

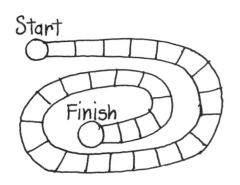   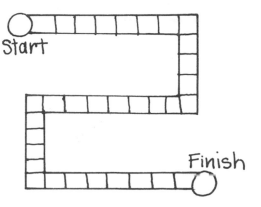

COUNTING GAMES

Skill: counting

Materials: none

Directions: 1. Tell the children you're going to play a game with them every day when it's time to come inside from the playground. You're going to count from 1 to 25 to see if they can get in line before you get to 25.

2. Raise your hand and start counting when it's time to go in. (You'll be amazed how the children will come running and join in counting with you.)

Adaptations:

* Let the children count the trees, riding toys, swings, balls, books, chairs, and everything else inside and outside on the playground.

* Ask the children to predict how many chairs, tables, or other objects there are. Then verify their answers by counting.

* Count aloud as the children swing, jump rope, bounce a ball, and do other exercises.

* Sing counting songs, such as "Ten Little Teddy Bears" and "Five Little Monkeys."

* Encourage the children to count out snacks, books, and other items as they hand them out.

* Count how many steps to the cafeteria, how many stairs by the front door, and so forth.

 **ALL ABOARD**

Skill:	numerical order

Materials:
* ✱ construction paper
* ✱ scissors, markers
* ✱ plastic storage bag or envelope

Directions:
1. Cut out a train engine from black construction paper.
2. Cut out all train cars from colored construction paper and print numerals from 0 to 10 on them.
3. Mix up the train cars, then ask the children to put them in order behind the engine.
4. Store in a plastic bag or envelope.

Adaptation:
* ✱ Print alphabet letters on the train cars and have the children put them in alphabetical order.

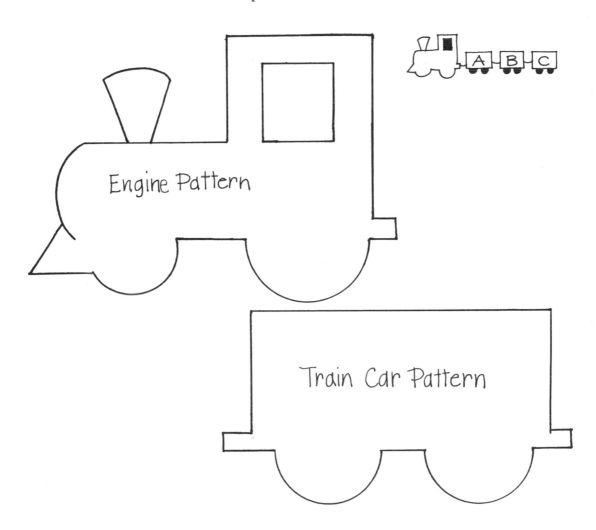

Engine Pattern

Train Car Pattern

HANG-UPS

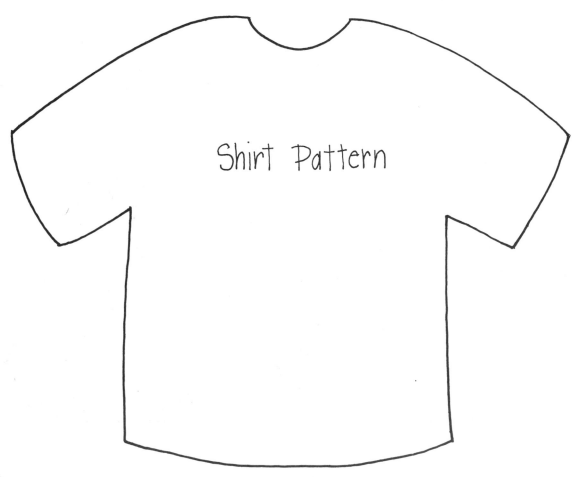

Skill: numerical order

Materials:
* construction paper
* spring clothespins
* markers, scissors, string or yarn

Directions:
1. Cut out 11 shirts using the pattern at the bottom of the page.
2. Print numerals from 0 to 10 on the shirts.
3. Tie a piece of string or yarn between two chairs.
4. Ask the children to hang up the shirts on the line in order using the clothespins. (Make sure the children do this in a left-to-right direction.)

Adaptations:
* Reinforce counting by tens by writing 10, 20, 30, 40, 50, 60, 70, 80, 90, 100 on the shirts.
* Ask the children, "What comes before 8?" "What numeral comes between 3 and 5?" "What comes after 2?" and so forth.

Shirt Pattern

MICE AND CHEESE

Skill:	number words
Materials:	* construction paper (gray and yellow) * markers * scissors * plastic storage bag or envelope
Directions:	1. Cut out ten gray mice using the pattern below. 2. Cut out ten pieces of cheese. 3. Write the number words from one to ten on the mice. Print numerals from 1 to 10 on the cheese. 4. Have the children match the appropriate mouse with the numeral on the cheese. 5. Store the pieces in a plastic bag or envelope.
Adaptation:	* Use this game for matching sets and numerals, upper- and lower-case letters, and math facts.

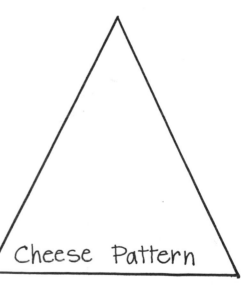

LEAF GRAPHS

How many?				
	1	2	3	4

Skill: comparing

Materials:
* large graph
* crayons

Directions:
1. Have each child find a leaf on the playground.
2. Graph how many of each leaf were found by coloring the graph.
3. Compare quantities.

Adaptations:
* Graph favorite outdoor game, animal, snack, toy, pet, weather condition, and so forth.
* Do a class graph called "All About Us." Let the children color in their eye color, skin (use multicultural crayons or markers), hair, the number of people in their family, and so on.

All About Us

Name	Hair	Skin	Eyes	Number in Family	Favorite Food	Number of Pets
Miguel				5		2
Yen				3		0

BEAR GRAPHS

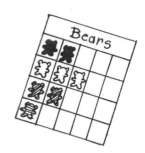

Skill: graphs

Materials:
* bear-shaped pasta dyed red, yellow, blue, and green (see "Pasta! Pasta!" activity for directions)
* plastic bags
* graphing cards made from 12" squares of cardboard
* ruler, markers

Directions:
1. Make graphing cards from the cardboard as shown below.
2. Mix up the pasta, then put a handful in each bag.
3. Give each child a bag of pasta and a graph.
4. Children can sort the pasta by color on the graph.
5. When they are finished, ask such questions as, "Which color has the most?" "Least?" "How many red bears do you have?" "How many green and blue bears together?" and so on.

Adaptations:
* Let the children sort teddy bear crackers of different colors and flavors in a similar manner.
* Use cereal mix and other mixed snacks for graphing, counting, and other math activities.

How many bears?							
	1	2	3	4	5	6	7
red							
blue							
yellow							
green							

LITTLE TO BIG

Skill: seriation

Materials: * sticks of varying lengths

Directions: 1. Have the children put the sticks in order from shortest to longest.

2. Begin with three or four sticks, then add more according to the children's abilities.

3. Ask questions such as "Which one is longest? How can you tell? Which one is shortest?"

Adaptations: * Let the children seriate leaves, blades of grass, rocks, flowers, and other natural objects. Ask the children to find the tallest tree on the playground, the shortest tree, widest bush, and so forth.

* Give the children play dough and ask them to make a snake. "Can you make one longer than that?" "Can you make one shorter?"

* Get paint chips from a paint store, cut them apart, and ask the children to seriate them by shade.

* Cut cardboard rollers, straws, ribbon, and other objects in varying lengths for the children to seriate.

© 1994 by The Center for Applied Research in Education

MEASURE UP

Skill: measurement

Materials: * yarn cut in varying lengths

Directions: 1. Give each child a piece of yarn and ask them to find something as long as their piece of yarn. Find something longer. Find something shorter.

2. Let them trade pieces of yarn. Is their new piece longer or shorter? Ask them to find something of the same length.

3. Use a standard unit, such as a block or shoe, to measure different things in the classroom or on the playground.

Adaptations:

* Make a ruler for each child from cardboard. Ask them to find something one inch long, four inches long, and so on.

* Older children will enjoy working in pairs to measure the size of the classroom, the distance to the front door, or the windows.

* Find out how long prehistoric dinosaurs were, then measure that distance on the playground. Measure the length of whales, elephants, and other animals.

COUPON CLIPPERS

Skill: sorting; money

Materials:
* file folder
* coupons from the newspaper or magazines
* scissors, markers, glue
* library pockets or envelopes

Directions:

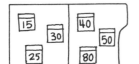

1. Glue four to eight library pockets to the file folder as shown.
2. Sort through coupons to determine the amount to write on the library pockets, then write those amounts with a marker.
3. Have the children take the coupons and place them in the pocket with the same amount.
4. Older children can add up how much money they can save. How much could they save if there were double coupons?

Adaptations:

* Let the children cut out the coupons or bring those from home that their family does not use.
* Ask the children to sort coupons by food and nonfood items, things that belong in the freezer or cupboard, and any other categories they can think of.
* Give the children a menu from a restaurant and $5.00. What would they like to order for that amount? Will they have any money left over? How much would it cost their family to go out to eat?
* Food cans and boxes can provide children with countless nutrition as well as math activities. What percentage of fat does the product have? How many calories per serving?

GO FISHING

Skill:	math facts

Materials:
* construction paper
* string or yarn
* markers, scissors
* paper clips
* horseshoe magnet
* stick

Directions:

1. Cut the fish from the pattern below out of construction paper. Use several different colors of paper.
2. On each fish print an addition or subtraction fact.
3. Attach a paper clip to the end of each fish. Tie the magnet to one end of a 3-foot piece of yarn, and then tie the other end to the stick.
4. Spread the fish out on the floor. One child at a time should take the fishing pole, place the magnet near the paper clip on a fish, and pretend to "catch" the fish. He or she must then tell the answer to the math problem.

Adaptation:
* Use this fishing pole for numeral recognition, letters, sight words, color identification, and other information.

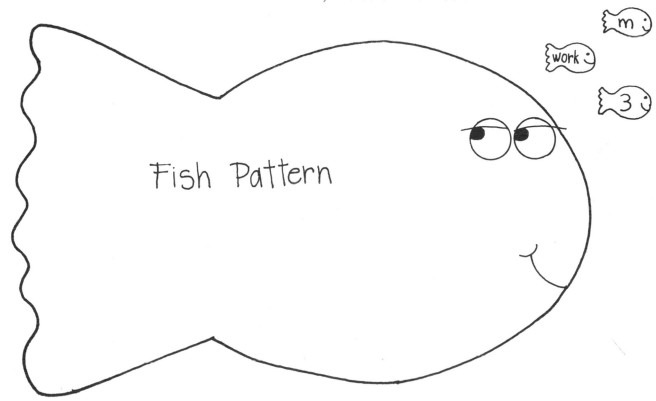

Fish Pattern

TOUCHDOWN

Skill: math facts

Materials:
  * brown construction paper
  * scissors, markers
  * plastic bag or envelope

Directions:

1. Cut out 20–30 footballs from brown construction paper using the pattern below.
2. Write math facts on the footballs.
3. Have the children sit in a circle. Hold up footballs one at a time and have the children put their arms in the air if they know the answer. When most of the children have their hands in the air, ask them to say the answer together. (This technique gives more children the opportunity to respond to the problem.)
4. Store the footballs in a plastic bag or envelope.

Adaptations:

  * Use the footballs for letter recognition, sight words, or other skills you are trying to teach.
  * Two or three children can play a game with the footballs. Put the footballs in a pile face down on the table or floor. The children then take turns turning over footballs. The first one to identify the information on the ball gets to keep it.

© 1994 by The Center for Applied Research in Education

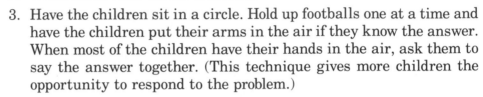

Football Pattern

RAINBOW PATHWAY

Skill: math facts

Materials:
* construction paper, white paper
* markers, scissors
* storage bag or envelope

Directions:
1. Cut out ten clouds from white paper.
2. Cut out ten rainbows from colored construction paper.
3. Write math facts on the rainbows, and the answers on the clouds.
4. Children match rainbows to the appropriate answer on the clouds.
5. Store in a plastic bag or envelope.

Adaptation:
* Match color words, number words, and other concepts with rainbows and clouds.

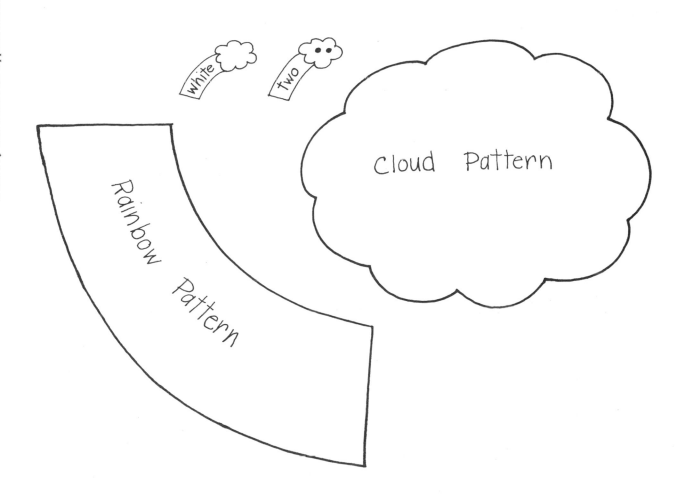

THUMBS-UP COMPUTER

Skill: math facts

Materials:
* * large cardboard box (approximately 3' × 2')
* * scissors or utility knife
* * markers
* * index cards

Directions:

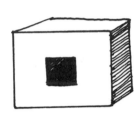

1. Cut one side off the box. On the opposite side cut a 4" square. Decorate the box around the square with markers to look like a computer.

2. Write math facts on the front of the index cards, then put the answer on the reverse side.

3. Set the computer on a child's desk or table. Let one child sit behind the computer to be the "computer genius." The other children sit in front of the computer.

4. The "computer genius" takes a card and reads the math problem on it to the rest of the group. You call on a child to provide the answer. If they answer correctly, the "computer genius" sticks his or her hand out of the hole and holds their thumb up. If the answer is incorrect, he or she puts their thumb down and someone else is allowed to answer the problem.

5. The game continues with the "computer genius" reinforcing the group with a "thumbs-up." (Allow other children to take turns playing "computer genius.")

Adaptation:
* * This game can be used for reinforcing many different skills.

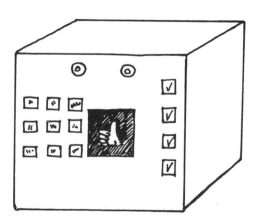

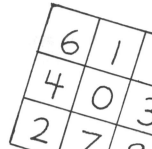

 NUMBO

Skill: math facts

Materials:
* cardboard cut in 9" squares
* markers, ruler
* flashcards of math facts
* game markers (dried beans, buttons, paper circles, cereal, and so forth)

Directions:
1. Mark cardboard squares into nine sections as shown. In each section print a numeral to correspond with the answers on your flashcards. (Try to make all the cards different.)
2. Give each child a card and at least nine markers.
3. Read one problem on a flashcard at a time. Children may cover up this numeral on their card if they have it.
4. The first child to cover all the numerals on his or her card yells "Numbo!"

Adaptations:
* Add twelve or more sections on the cards and more difficult numerals for older children.
* Make up word problems and have the children cover up the answer on their cards.
* You can make a similar game called "Alpha" by using alphabet letters on the cards. Use this game for letter recognition or for reviewing sounds.

ALPHA			
E	J	P	I
L	A	G	D
O	F	R	M
C	W	K	H

POKE AND PEEK

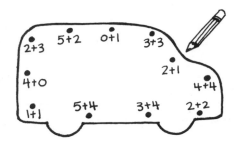

Skill: math facts

Materials:
* posterboard
* scissors, hole punch, markers
* pencil

Directions:

1. Take a sheet of posterboard approximately 8" × 11". Cut out a simple shape, such as an apple, car, beehive, tree, or ball.
2. With the hole punch, cut 10–15 holes around the outside of the shape.
3. Write a math fact near each hole. On the reverse side, write the answer to the math fact near the hole.
4. Outline the shape with marker and decorate.
5. Two children can play this game. One child holds the card and takes a pencil and pokes it in a hole. He or she reads the math problem and says the answer. Another child sits opposite looking at the back of the card. The answer can be checked by the numeral next to where the pencil point is.

Adaptations:
* Use this game to reinforce antonyms, synonyms, and so on.
* Let the children work on letter recognition, numerals, sight words, and other skills with a Poke-and-Peek game.
* A pizza cardboard also works well for a Poke-and-Peek game.

front

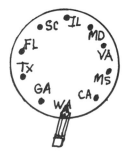

back

MR. CHIPPER

Skill: math facts

Materials:
* potato chip canister
* posterboard
* construction paper
* scissors
* markers

Directions:

front

back

front	back
5-2	
6-3	3
1-1	3
7-4	0
9-0	3
4-2	2

1. Wrap the outside of the can with construction paper and decorate with markers.
2. Cut a slit in the plastic lid.
3. Trace around the pattern on the following page from posterboard and cut it out. (Construction paper will also work if you laminate it.) Decorate the circle like a person.
4. On the front side of the cardboard insert, write math facts. On the back write the answers to the problems.
5. The child inserts the cardboard through the slit into the can. He or she then slowly pulls the cardboard slit out, answering the problem and then checking their answer on the back. (Two children can also play this game. One child calls out the answer while the other child checks the back.)

Adaptation:

* Sight words, antonyms, contractions, and other information can be reviewed in this game format.

Mr. Chipper Pattern

114

"EGG"-CITING EGG CARTON MATH

Skill: addition facts

Materials:

* egg carton
* markers
* dry beans

Directions:

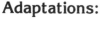

1. Print numerals from 1 to 6 in the bottom section on each side of the egg carton.
2. Take two beans, put them in the egg carton, close the lid, and shake them up.
3. Open the carton and add the two numerals where the beans landed.

Adaptations:

* Let the children play with three, four, or five beans and add the total number.
* Write larger numerals in the bottom of each section for older children.
* Have the children multiply numerals instead of add.
* For younger children, ask them to count out sets of beans, dry cereal, or other small objects in each section.
* Hide sets of beans from 1–12 in plastic eggs. Children open the eggs, count the beans, then match the amount with the numeral in the egg carton.
* Print a letter in the bottom of each section. Using the egg pattern, draw pictures of objects beginning with each sound on the egg. Children match eggs with appropriate lettered sections.
* Color the bottom of each section, then cut out eggs of matching colors. Children match eggs to the appropriate color in the carton.

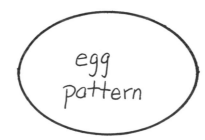

egg pattern

MATH STRETCH

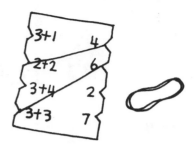

Skill: math facts

Materials:
* posterboard or cardboard scraps
* rubber bands
* markers

Directions:

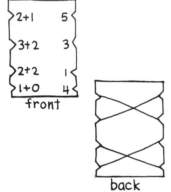

1. Cut cardboard into a 5½" × 8" rectangle.
2. Cut little triangular niches along opposite sides of the cardboard as shown.
3. Print an addition fact close to the indented point on the left side. Print the answers by the indentations on the right side.
4. Turn the card over and match the correct facts and answers with a straight line.
5. Give the child several rubber bands. The child matches the math problems and answers by stretching the rubber band through the grooves. When they are finished, they can turn the card over to see if their rubber bands match the drawn lines.

Adaptations:

* This game can be used for matching like shapes, pictures, rhyming words, upper- and lower-case letters, states and capitals, and almost any information.
* Add more grooves to the sides of each card depending on the age of the children.

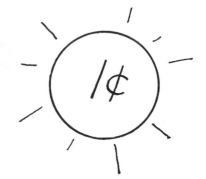

SECRET PENNIES

Skill: missing addend

Materials: * margarine tub
                      * pennies

Directions: 1. Begin with three pennies. Turn the margarine tub upside down and lay the pennies on top. Have the children count the pennies with you. "They are magic because there will always be three."

                      2. Tell the children to close their eyes while you take some pennies and hide them under the tub. (Take two pennies and put them underneath.)

                      3. Ask the children to open their eyes and guess how many pennies are under the tub. Let one child lift the tub to verify their guess.

                      4. Continue hiding different amounts with different sets of pennies.

Adaptations: * Let the children play this game in pairs, hiding pennies for their friends to guess.

                      * Use increasing amounts of pennies depending on the age of the children.

                      * Use blocks, pencils, crayons, and other classroom objects and hide them under a shoebox.

                      * Have the children make up number stories or write equations to go along with this activity.

 **SEASONAL IDEAS**

Make math games that relate to various holidays and seasons.

Sort the leaves.

Seriate the pumpkins.

Reproduce a pattern to string on the tree.

Count candy canes.

Add valentines.

Match envelopes and cards one-to-one.

Match sets and numerals with kite tails.

Sequence numerals on shamrocks.

Count eggs in a basket.

Measure flower stems.

SECTION 3

Science Surprises

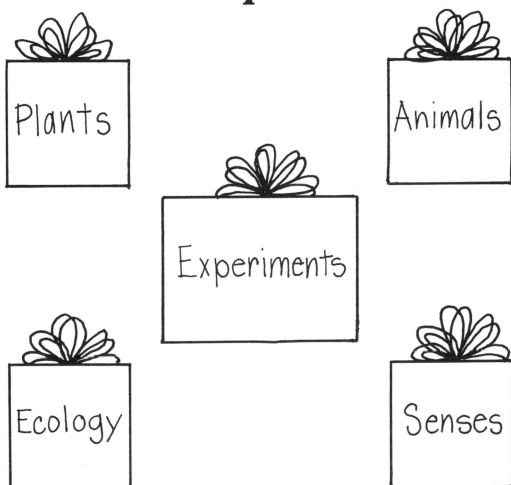

Surprise yourself and your students with the following science experiments and activities. From dancing raisins to seedy socks and the earth patrol, children will use their senses and minds as they explore their world around them.

The science experiments in this section have been written so that children can use them independently at a learning center, or they can be copied on a poster or chart for group activities.

 # DANCING RAISINS

Skill: observing; predicting

Materials:
* small box of raisins
* clear carbonated soda (ginger ale, lemon, and so forth)
* clear glass

Directions:

1. Fill the glass halfway with the soda.
2. Drop five or six raisins in the glass.
3. Watch carefully to see what the raisins will do.
4. What makes the raisins go up and down? What happens when the air bubbles form around the raisins?

 # MAGIC PENNIES

Skill: experimenting; observing

Materials:
* pennies (old, dull ones work best)
* vinegar
* table salt
* cup and spoon

Directions:

1. Put ½ cup vinegar in the cup.
2. Add one tablespoon salt and stir well.
3. Drop the pennies in the cup, then stir them around as you count to 25.
4. Take out the pennies and rinse them in water.
5. What happened to the pennies? What made them shiny?

 **MYSTERY MESS**

Skill: experimenting

Materials:
* cornstarch
* water
* food coloring
* measuring cup, bowl, spoon

Directions:
1. Put one cup cornstarch in the bowl.
2. Slowly stir in about ½ cup water. (You may need to add a little more water to make it the right consistency.)
3. Add a few drops of food coloring to the mixture.
4. Try to pick up your mystery mess and play with it. How is it like a solid? How is it like a liquid?

PEPPER SCATTER

Skill: observing; experimenting

Materials:
* pepper
* liquid detergent
* clear bowl, water

Directions:
1. Fill the bowl with water.
2. Sprinkle the pepper on top.
3. Squirt a drop of detergent in the middle of the bowl.
4. What happens to the pepper?

Adaptation:
* Pour a cup of milk in a pie pan and let it sit to room temperature. Squirt several different colors of food coloring down the sides of the pan. Then squirt a little detergent in the middle of the pan. What happens to the colors? (You may have to wiggle the pan just a little to make the colors start moving.)

121

VOLCANIC ACTION

Skill: experimenting; observing

Materials:
* baking soda
* vinegar
* red food coloring
* cup, spoon, shallow pan

Directions:
1. Set the cup inside the pan.
2. Put ½ cup vinegar in the cup. Add a few drops of red food coloring.
3. Add two tablespoons baking soda to the vinegar and stir. (CAUTION: Have an adult supervise this.)
4. Watch out for your volcano!
5. Find out what causes a real volcano to erupt.

Adaptation:
* Take a soda bottle and a large balloon. (Blow up the balloon several times so it will be easier to inflate.) Draw a silly face on the balloon with markers. Put ½ cup vinegar in the bottle, then put several tablespoons baking soda in the balloon with a spoon. Insert the balloon over the top of the bottle and watch what happens to the balloon.

CRYSTAL GARDEN

Skill: experimenting; communicating

Materials:
* baby food jar or pie pan
* charcoal
* salt
* bluing
* ammonia (CAUTION: carefully supervise this!)
* food coloring
* cup, spoon, measuring spoons

Directions:
1. Put a piece of charcoal in the jar or pan.
2. Mix the following ingredients in a cup, then pour the mixture over the charcoal: one tablespoon salt, one tablespoon water, one tablespoon bluing, one teaspoon ammonia.
3. Sprinkle a few drops of food coloring on top.
4. Set the crystal garden in a safe place and watch it grow. Describe your experiment to a friend.

MAGNETIC POWER

Skill:	experimenting; predicting
Materials:	* magnet
	* box of junk (paper clips, safety pins, tissue, plastic toys, nails, toothpicks)
	* piece of cardboard
	* cup of water

Directions:

1. Take the magnet and try to pick up each object in the junk box.
2. Make a pile of things that the magnet attracts and a pile of the things it does not attract. How are the things the magnet attracts alike?
3. Put a paper clip in a cup of water. Will the magnet pick it up through the water?
4. Put a paper clip on top of the cardboard. Put the magnet under the cardboard and see if you can move the paper clip.

Adaptations:

* Take the magnet out on the playground and see if you can find things it will attract.
* You can make your own magnet. Get a strong magnet and a 2" steel nail. Quickly rub the magnet over the nail 100 times, then try to pick up a straight pin or a paper clip.

 # WATER MAGNIFIER

Skill:	observing; experimenting
Materials:	* styrofoam meat tray or styrofoam plate
	* clear plastic wrap
	* tape
	* tiny objects (coin, flower)

Directions:

1. Cut a circle in the middle of the styrofoam plate or food tray.
2. Tape clear plastic wrap across the top.
3. Pour water on top to cover the circle.
4. Look through the water at tiny objects. What happens to them?

Adaptation:

* Fill a clear glass with water. Put a pencil in the glass and look at it from the side. Does the pencil look broken? What happens when you stick your finger in the water?

REFLECTOR CARDS

Skill: experimenting

Materials:
* cardboard scraps (cut up empty food boxes)
* aluminum foil

Directions:
1. Cut a piece of cardboard about the size of your hand. It can be a circle, triangle, square, or rectangle.
2. Take a piece of aluminum foil twice as big as your shape and wrap it around the shape with the shiny side out.
3. Go outside and hold the reflector card in the sun. Can you make the sun reflect from the card? Will this work on a cloudy day?

Adaptation:
* Put your card in the sun. How does it feel? Put it in the shade. How does it feel? Why does it get hot in the sun?

 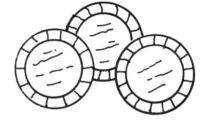

COLOR PADDLES

Skill: experimenting; observing

Materials:
* 6 paper plates
* clear red, yellow, and blue cellophane (acetate report covers or colored overhead projector sheets will also work)
* stapler, scissors

Directions:

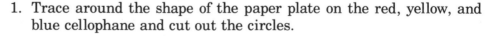

1. Trace around the shape of the paper plate on the red, yellow, and blue cellophane and cut out the circles.
2. Cut the middle section out of each paper plate.
3. Put each colored circle between two paper plate rims and staple in place.
4. Hold up two circles together and see what new color you can make.

Adaptations:
* Take the color paddles out on the playground and experiment with them. What happens when you look at things through them?
* Hang up sheets of colored acetate on windows or the playground fence for the children to look through.

MIRROR, MIRROR

Skill: observing; predicting

Materials:
* small mirror
* paper, pencil

Directions: 1. Place the mirror next to the following shapes.

Can you make the whole tree?

Where's the rest of the cookie?

How many legs does the bug have?

How long can you make the jump rope?

Who will play with me?

Help me find my other mitten.

2. Take a sheet of paper. Make your own designs and half-pictures that you can reflect in the mirror.

Adaptation: * Write your name. Then hold the mirror next to it. Why does it appear backwards? Can you write your name so that it looks correct in the mirror?

HAIRY CREATURES

Skill: experimenting; communicating

Materials:
* grass seed (rye works best)
* potting soil
* plain paper cups
* markers

Directions:

Days

1. Draw a face on the cup with markers.
2. Fill the cup halfway with soil.
3. Sprinkle grass seed on the dirt.
4. Water the seeds with an empty spray bottle, then set the cup in a sunny window.
5. Watch the seeds grow hair on your cup. Graph how many days it takes your grass to grow.
6. When the hair gets too long, give it a haircut with scissors.

Adaptation:

* Plant several different cups with grass seed. Then put one in a dark closet, don't water one, put one in an airtight container, and don't use soil with another. Record what happens to each cup.

WHAT'S UP?

Skill: experimenting; observing

Materials:
* 2 cups of water
* red and blue food coloring
* 2 stalks of celery

Directions:

1. Put several drops of red food coloring in one cup. Add blue food coloring to the other cup.
2. Put a stalk of celery in each cup and observe it for several days.
3. What happens to the tips of the leaves? Why?

Adaptations:

* Try this experiment with white carnations, daffodils, and other flowers.
* Split a stalk of celery halfway up from the bottom. Put one end in the blue food coloring and the other end in red food coloring. Observe what happens.

126

JACK'S BEANSTALK

Skill: experimenting; observing

Materials:
* clear cup or jar
* paper towel
* sand or soil
* dry lima beans

Directions:

1. Fold the paper towel to fit inside the jar.
2. Put sand or soil inside the paper towel.
3. Drop several beans between the paper towel and the jar.
4. Water the beans well and place them in a sunny spot.
5. How many days before you see a root? A stem?

Adaptations:

* You can do a similar experiment with a sandwich bag. Fold a paper towel to fit inside the bag. Staple a line across the bag about halfway from the bottom. Insert a few beans, water, and hang on the bulletin board to grow.

* Plan a seed snack where you eat popcorn, sunflower seeds, or pumpkin seeds.

* Go on a seed hunt in your kitchen and see how many seeds you can find. Plant popcorn kernels, apple seeds, orange seeds, avocados, and other seeds.

* Place a sponge in a shallow pan of water. Sprinkle birdseed on the sponge and water daily. (It's fun to cut the sponge in a shape for a holiday, such as a shamrock or heart.)

* Soak lima beans in a wet paper towel overnight. Then split them open in the morning to find a baby plant.

* Start a mini-nursery in a cardboard egg carton. Fill each section with dirt and a few seeds. Water, then transplant to a larger container or garden when the nursery begins to grow (a few inches).

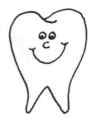

HAPPY TEETH

Skill: experimenting; predicting

Materials:
* 4 eggs
* clear cups
* water, cola, tea, coffee (1 cup each)

Directions:

1. Fill each cup half full with the water, cola, tea, and coffee. (Label the cups accordingly.)
2. Carefully submerge one egg in each cup.
3. After several days remove the eggs from the cups. Examine the enamel on each egg. What liquids stained the eggs? How are your teeth like the eggs? What drinks will stain your teeth?

Adaptations:
* Brush the eggs carefully with a toothbrush and toothpaste. What happens?
* Invite a dentist to speak to your class about caring for teeth.

SAME AND DIFFERENT

Skill: predicting

Materials:
* 1 brown egg
* 1 white egg
* 2 clear cups

Directions:

1. Gently hold one egg in each hand. How are the eggs alike? How are they different?
2. Crack the brown egg into one cup. Crack the white egg in the other cup. Are they the same inside?
3. How are people like these eggs?

Adaptation:
* Cook something with the eggs, such as "green eggs and ham." Scramble the eggs, then add a few drops of green food coloring and some diced ham. Cook in a little butter. Mmmm!

BIRD FEEDER

Skill: observing

Materials:
* plastic milk jug
* birdseed
* scissors, yarn

Directions:
1. Cut a hole in the side of the milk jug with scissors.
2. Punch two holes in the top and tie on a piece of yarn for a hanger.
3. Put a cup of birdseed in the bottom of the jug, then hang it in a tree.
4. Add a small stick for a perch.
5. Be a bird watcher! Can you name the birds that come to the feeder?

Adaptations:
* Go the library and check out a book that will help you learn the names of some of the birds on your playground.
* Here are some other bird feeders you can make:

String cereal on a pipe cleaner.

Put honey on a pinecone, then sprinkle with seed.

Spread peanut butter on a large pretzel or toilet paper dowel and sprinkle with seed.

Cut shapes from stale bread and decorate with honey and birdseed.

Weave bits of yarn, hay, and string in a berry basket for birds to use for building nests.

NATURE WATCHERS

Skill: observing

Materials:
* 2 cardboard toilet paper dowels
* tape or stapler
* hole punch, yarn or string
* crayons or markers

Directions:
1. Tape or staple the two dowels together.
2. Punch a hole in the top of each dowel. Then tie a piece of string through the holes. (Make sure the string is long enough to go over your head easily.)
3. Decorate the binoculars with markers or crayons.
4. Go outside and look for animals, plants, birds, and beautiful things in nature.

© 1994 by The Center for Applied Research in Education

 # CRITTER CAGE

Skill: observing

Materials:
* plastic bottle (half-gallon milk jug works well)
* old panty hose
* scissors
* twisty tie

Directions:

1. Cut two or three windows in your bottle with scissors.
2. Put some sticks, leaves, and grass in the bottom of the bottle.
3. Cut off one leg from the panty hose and stretch it over the bottle.
4. Catch a little bug, caterpillar, lizard, or other critter and gently put it in the bottle.
5. Use a twisty tie at the top so that it doesn't get out.
6. Observe the critter for a little while, then put it back where you found it.

 **WHIRLY BIRD**

Skill: experimenting; observing

Materials:
* construction paper
* scissors
* paper clips

Directions:
1. Trace around the pattern on the following page and cut it out.
2. Fold over the bottom sections and attach a paper clip at the end.
3. Fold down the top flaps in opposite directions.
4. Hold the whirly bird up high, then let it go. Whee!
5. Take it out on the playground and let it go from the top of a climber.

Adaptations:
* Fold both flaps in the same direction and let it go. Will it fly? Will it work without the paper clip?
* Make paper airplanes and have a contest to see who can design one that will fly the farthest.
* Take two sheets of paper. Wad one up into a ball. Now stand on a chair, holding the plain sheet of paper in one hand and the paper wad in the other hand. If you let them both go at the same time, which one do you think will fall faster? Why? Try it and see what happens.
* To make a flying fish, trace around the pattern below. Cut it out, insert the tabs, hold it up in the air, then let it spin.

Flying Fish Pattern

cut   cut

WHIRLY BIRD PATTERN

Trace onto construction paper and cut out. Fold on the dotted lines and secure ends with a paper clip. Bend each of the propellers in the opposite direction. Hold up high, then let go!

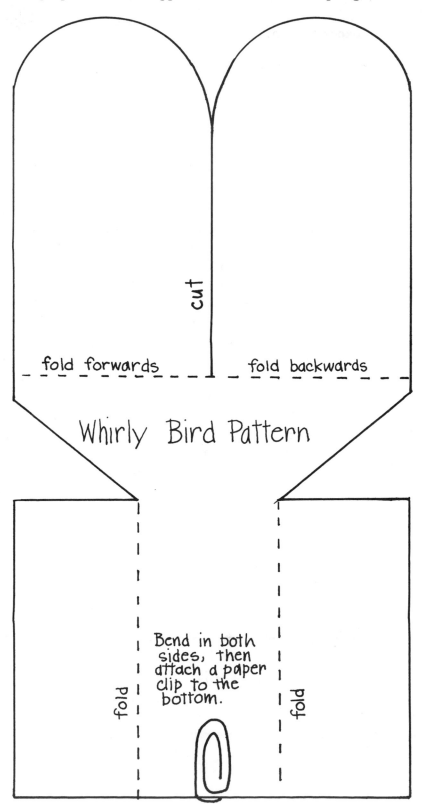

cut

fold forwards   fold backwards

Whirly Bird Pattern

fold

fold

Bend in both sides, then attach a paper clip to the bottom.

OCEAN IN A JAR

Skill: experimenting

Materials:
* clear plastic bottle with cap
* vegetable oil
* food coloring
* water

Directions:
1. Fill the bottle ⅔ full with water.
2. Add a few drops of food coloring.
3. Fill the bottle almost to the top with oil, then screw on the top. (You might want to put glue around the top so it doesn't leak.)
4. Turn the jar on its side and gently roll it to make waves.

Adaptations:
* Fill a plastic bottle with clear Karo® corn syrup. Put several small objects in the bottle and observe how each one floats to the bottom.
* Fill a bottle with water. Add a few drops food coloring and some glitter and shake it.
* Put a few tablespoons of clear Karo® corn syrup in a plastic bottle. Add a few drops of food coloring, screw on the top, and move the bottle all around while watching the syrup cover the inside.
* Put some dirt in the bottom of a plastic bottle, then fill it up with water. Shake it, then let it sit. Watch the dirt settle to the bottom.
* Pour a little sand in a plastic bottle. Add water, blue food coloring, and some shells. Shake it, then observe what happens.
* Fill a bottle ⅓ full with water. Add a few drops food coloring and a squirt of detergent. Screw on the top, then shake it to make bubbles.

colored water and glitter

dirt and water

Karo® corn syrup and food coloring

water, soap, and food coloring

AMATEUR ARCHAEOLOGISTS

Skill: observing; communicating

Materials:
* sand shovel or large spoon
* plastic container
* magnifying glass
* tweezers
* newspapers or large flat pan

Directions:

1. Go outside and dig up some dirt under a bush or tree.
2. Spread the dirt out on a newspaper or large flat pan.
3. Use the magnifying glass to look at the dirt. What do you see? Can you tell a story from the bits and pieces of things you find in the dirt?
4. Use the tweezers to separate the leaves, rocks, sticks, and other objects you find.

Adaptations:

Iowa

* Collect soil samples from different areas on your playground or your yard. Put them in plastic bags and label them. How is the soil different?
* Ask grandparents, friends, and relatives to send you soil samples from where they live. Compare the different types of soil we have in different areas of the country.
* Make your own fossils by imprinting shells, rocks, leaves, and other objects in clay or plaster of Paris.

 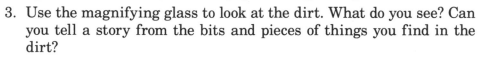

TEENY TINY COLLECTION

Skill: classifying

Materials:
* egg carton
* pipe cleaner

Directions:

1. Cut the egg carton in half. Insert the pipe cleaner in the top to make a handle.
2. Take a nature walk or go out on the playground and find a tiny item that will fit in each compartment.

IT MAKES SENSE I

Skill: sense of touch

Materials:
* old socks
* ball, spoon, crayon, block, toy car, penny, and other small objects

Directions:
1. Take several pairs of old socks. Put a different object in the toe of each sock, then tie at the top.
2. Mix up the socks, then let the children guess what is in each one by feeling it.

Adaptations:

* Take off your shoes and sit at a table. Try to identify different objects with your feet as a friend places them under the table where you can't see them.
* Take a large plastic cup. Stretch an old sock over it. Put different items in the bottom and let the children take turns reaching in and describing the object. (Look for unusual items, such as a scouring pad, natural sponge, charcoal, and so on.)

 # IT MAKES SENSE II

Skill: sense of hearing

Materials:
* 10 film containers (any place that develops film will give these to you free)
* rice, beans, pennies, paper clips, salt

Directions:

1. Put a little rice in two film containers, add beans to two, pennies to two, paper clips to two, and salt to two.
2. Put the tops on the canisters and mix them up.
3. Try to match the containers that have the same items by matching their sounds.

Adaptations:

* Put matching stickers on the bottoms of the canisters so the children can self-check.
* You can make a similar game with plastic eggs. Get 12 eggs and put like items in two eggs. Match the eggs with like sounds in an egg carton.
* Hide a music box or portable radio out of sight in the room. Then let the children take turns finding it.

135

IT MAKES SENSE III

Skill:	sense of smell
Materials:	* film containers
	* cotton balls
	* peanut butter, coffee, oregano, cinnamon, bubble gum, vinegar, baby powder, lemon slice, chocolate, or other items that have a distinguishing smell
Directions:	1. Take five film containers and put one of the above items in each.
	2. Put several cotton balls on the top of each so you can't see what's inside.
	3. Mix up the containers, then let the children guess what each one is.
Adaptation:	* Make your own spice cards to smell. Cut 3" squares of cardboard. Spread a little rubber cement on each, then sprinkle with different spices.

IT MAKES SENSE IV

Skill:	sense of taste
Materials:	* paper plates and napkins
Directions:	1. Ask each child in the room to bring something to school to eat for a tasting party. Discuss the importance of bringing healthy foods, such as fruits, vegetables, breads, and cheese. (Write a note to the parents about it and ask them to have it cut up into the number of pieces you will need for everyone in the room to have a taste.)
	2. Which foods taste sweet? Salty? Which foods are hard? Soft?
	3. Do a graph of favorite foods.
Adaptation:	* Plan a white taste test. You will need five small bowls and five spoons. Put a little flour, powdered sugar, baking powder, salt, and sugar in the bowls. After washing your hands, sprinkle a little of each in your palm with the spoon. Can you tell what it is by looking at it? Use your tongue to taste it and see if you can tell what it is.

SORTING BOX

Skill: classifying

Materials:
* shoebox
* tape, scissors
* cardboard
* magazine pictures of things you would find "inside" or "outside" the home

Directions:
1. Cut a piece of cardboard to fit down the middle of the shoebox and tape it in place.
2. Label one side of the box "inside" and draw a picture clue of a house. Label the other side "outside" and draw a picture clue of a sun.
3. Let the children sort the magazine pictures according to whether they would find it inside or outside.

Adaptation:
* Ask the children to sort pictures of other objects, such as:

    real and pretend
    living and nonliving
    healthy foods and junk foods
    things that are safe to play with or not safe
    summer and winter
    big and little
    up or down
    land or water

CLOUD WATCH

Skill: observing

Materials:
* a blue sky with fluffy clouds

Directions:
1. Have the children look in the sky. "Do you see any clouds that remind you of animals or other objects?"
2. Continue looking for "pictures" in the clouds.

Adaptations:
* Take blankets or carpet squares to lie on while you look at the clouds.
* Read *It Looked Like Spilt Milk* by Charles G. Shaw.
* Draw pictures with white chalk on blue paper, or use white paint on blue paper.
* Take a nap on the playground.

 # THERMOMETER

Skill: communicating

Materials:
* large outdoor thermometer

Directions:
1. Place the thermometer in a prominent place on the playground where you can also view it from your room.
2. Explain what the numerals mean and count by tens on the thermometer.
3. Each day before you go out to play, have the children read the thermometer and predict how it will feel outside.

Adaptations:
* Keep a monthly graph of the temperature each day.
* Put a rain gauge or plastic jar on your playground. Measure and record the rainfall. Examine the water. Is it clean? Why or why not?

EVAPORATION

Skill: experimenting; predicting

Materials:
* paper towels
* pans of water

Directions:
1. Give each child a paper towel. Have them put it in the water, wring it out, then hang it out to dry.
2. Check on the towels until they dry. Where did the water go?

Adaptations:
* Set out a jar of water in a covered area on the playground. Record the water level every day. How long does it take the water to evaporate?
* Place a wet towel in the sun and one in the shade. What happens? Why?
* Spray water on each child's hand. Have them run around for a few minutes. Where did the water go?
* Give each child a cup with an ice cube in it and see who can melt their's fastest.

 # HUMAN SUNDIAL

Skill: observing

Materials:
* a sunny day
* chalk

Directions:
1. Have one child face north at 9:00 in the morning. Mark where he or she is standing and the shadow of their head and write the time beside it.
2. Have the child stand in the same spot and mark his or her shadow at various times in the school day.

Adaptations:
* Why does the shadow change when the person is standing still?
* Let the children trace around each other's shadows with chalk on the sidewalk.

139

 **"KINDER" GARDEN**

Skill:	experimenting; observing; communicating
Materials:	* child-size garden tools
	* seeds
	* planting soil
	* area on the playground with a lot of sun

Directions:

1. Mark off the area for your garden with rocks, railroad ties, or bricks.
2. Ask a parent with a roto-tiller to work up your soil.
3. Let the children spread the planting soil and work it in with their tools.
4. Make rows and let the children plant their seeds.
5. Involve the children in weeding, watering, and caring for the plants.
6. Let the children harvest, wash, cook, and eat their produce.

Adaptations:

* Make a graph to record plant growth.
* Make a scarecrow for your garden by stuffing old clothes with straw and leaves. Make a head from pantyhose and add a hat.
* Plant a garden in a plastic pool or sandbox in which holes have been made for drainage.
* Fill an old wagon or wheelbarrow with dirt for a garden.
* Start your own compost pile on the playground.
* Try an experiment to see which objects are biodegradable. "Plant" paper, styrofoam, egg shells, leaves, aluminum foil, and other items. (Label them when you plant them.) Dig them up after three or four weeks to see which ones have decomposed.

CLASS TREE

Skill: observing; communicating

Materials:
* large tree on your playground

Directions:
1. Explain to the children that your class is going to "adopt" a tree on the playground. You will all name it, love it, and care for it.
2. Go on the playground and find that special tree. Name it. Hug it. "How does it feel?" "How does it smell?" "Can you hear it?"
3. Draw pictures of the tree and let the children dictate stories about it. Put them together to make a class book.
4. Observe changes in the tree during different seasons.

Adaptations:
* Decorate the tree with bird feeders in the winter.
* Read *The Giving Tree* by Shel Silverstein.
* Take photographs of the tree during different seasons.

SEEDY SOCKS

Skill: experimenting

Materials:
* old socks
* self-locking plastic bags

Directions:
1. Put an old pair of socks on over your shoes.
2. Take a nature walk through some woods or a field.
3. When you return to the room, put the socks in plastic bags and dampen with water.
4. Seal the bags and hang in the window.
5. Observe the bags and see what grows.

Hint: This activity works best in the late summer or early fall when many plants have gone to seed.

141

DISCOVERY WALKS

Skill: observing

Materials: none

Directions:
1. Take children on a feeling walk.
2. Let them touch various objects in nature and describe how they feel.
3. Have them close their eyes and try to identify an object in their hands using their sense of touch.
4. "What things do you like to feel?" "What things do you not like to feel?" "What do your feet like to feel?"

Adaptations:
* Take a listening walk where children close their eyes and identify sounds in their environment.
* Take a smelling walk and use your noses. What smells good? What smells bad?
* How about a "duck walk" with umbrellas in the rain?

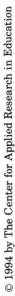

 # TREASURE BOX

Skill: collecting; classifying

Materials:
* detergent box with handle

Directions:
1. Let children collect various items, such as rocks, leaves, and nuts.
2. Let children sort objects, count them, describe, and compare.

EARTH PATROL

Skill: conserving

Materials: * empty cereal box or food box
                      * thick yarn, string, or ribbon
                      * hole punch, scissors

Directions: 1. Cut the top off the box. Punch a hole near the top on each side.
                      2. Tie a piece of yarn or string through the holes. (It will be 18"–24" depending on the size of the child.)
                      3. Put the bag over your shoulder, go outside, and pick up trash. (Discuss things that are not safe to pick up before you do this.)
                      4. Say this rap as you snap your fingers:

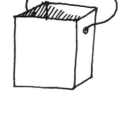

> Well, bless my soul.
> I'm on the Earth Patrol.
> I'm going to work all day
> To throw the trash away.
> The planet earth, you see,
> Belongs to you and me.
> It's our habitat.
> Well, how do you like that?

  JUNK SCULPTURES

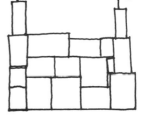

Skill: creativity

Materials: * empty cardboard containers
                      * junk
                      * masking tape, glue, scissors

Directions: 1. Ask the children and their parents to save food boxes and other containers for a week.
                      2. Let the children create houses, sculptures, inventions, or whatever else from the junk.

Adaptations: * Make a list of all the materials you can recycle.
                      * Start a recycling center in your classroom or school.
                      * Make a list of everything in your home or school that is made from recycled materials.

143

NATURE SCAVENGER HUNT

Skill: classifying

Materials: * paper bags

Directions: 1. Divide the children into small groups. Give each group a bag and
                       the list below.

CAN YOU FIND?

something green
something alive (but not an animal or bug)
something dead (but not an animal or bug)
something that smells good
something smaller than you
something older than you
something the size of your thumb
something that feels rough
something that feels soft
something that is beautiful
something that does not belong there
(Please pick it up and throw it in the trash can.)

---

2. Let the children hunt around until they find all the items. The first
   team to find everything wins.

Adaptation: * Do this as a large-group activity or individually.

Arts and Crafts

Creativity will soar with these art ideas in the classroom and out on the playground. Children will feel success and be delighted as they paint, glue, mold, and construct.

 MUD PAINTING

Skill: creativity; comparing

Materials:
* plastic containers
* old paintbrushes
* shovels
* water
* paper
* soil

Directions:
1. Collect soil samples from several different areas on your playground and put them in the plastic containers. Compare them. How are they alike and different?
2. Add water to the dirt to make mud.
3. Paint a picture with the paintbrush or with your fingers.

Adaptations:
* Do handprints and footprints with the mud. Attach this poem for a gift:

> "Here is a handprint made for you
> This Happy Mother's Day.
>   (holiday)
> It is one you can always keep
> And not have to wash away."

* Let the children paint a large mural with the mud.

 NATURE PAINTING

Skill: creativity

Materials:
* pine needles
* feathers
* sticks, leaves
* paint and shallow containers
* large sheets of paper
* clothespins or tape

Directions:
1. Attach the paper to a fence or wall with clothespins or tape.
2. Dip pine needles, feathers, and other objects in the paint and brush across the paper.

SCRAPE ART

Skill: creativity

Materials:
* paper
* masking tape
* newspaper
* tempera paints
* squirt bottles (ketchup, mustard, and so on)
* 3" × 12" strip of corrugated cardboard

Directions:
1. Cover the ground and table with newspaper.
2. Put tempera paint in squirt bottles. (Two or three colors will be plenty.)
3. Squirt paint at the top of the paper. (If you don't have squirt bottles, simply spoon tempera to the top of the paper.)
4. Take the cardboard strip, place it at the top of the page, and "scrape" off excess paint onto the newspaper.
5. Turn the paper all around and look for pictures, animals, and other objects in the design.

SCRIBBLE DESIGNS

Skill: creativity

Materials:
* butcher paper
* tape
* crayons
* rubber bands

Directions:
1. Tape large sheets of paper to a table or a wall.
2. Take three or four crayons and put a rubber band around them to make a bundle.
3. Let the children scribble on the paper with the crayon bundles.

Adaptation:
* Provide music while the children draw.

SQUIRT PAINTING

Skill: creativity

Materials:
* 2–4 empty spray bottles (glass cleaners, hair spritzer, and so forth)
* food coloring
* large sheets of paper or butcher paper
* clothespins or tape

Directions:
1. Fill the bottles halfway with water and add a different food coloring (five or six drops) to each one.
2. Attach large sheets of paper to a fence or wall with clothespins or tape.
3. Let the children spray the colored water onto the paper.

Adaptations:
* This makes great wrapping paper or can be used as background paper on the bulletin board.
* Use two primary colors (red, blue, or yellow) and let the children "discover" the secondary color they make.

© 1994 by The Center for Applied Research in Education

FLY SWATTER PAINTING

Skill: creativity

Materials:
* fly swatters
* paint, paper plates
* large sheets of paper
* clothespins or tape

Directions:
1. Tape or clothespin paper to the fence.
2. Pour a small amount of paint on a paper plate or shallow pan.
3. Let the children dip the fly swatter in the paint, then "swat" it on the paper.

Adaptation:
* Use large butcher paper for this project.

GARDEN ART

Skill: creativity; eye/hand coordination

Materials:
* dried flower petals and leaves
* paper
* glue

Directions:
1. Encourage the children to collect flowers and leaves and dry them. (Rose petals work especially well.)
2. Let the children arrange the dried petals and leaves on their paper, then glue them in place.

NATURE BRACELET

Skill: creativity

Materials:
* masking tape

Directions:
1. Before taking a nature walk, put a piece of masking tape on each child's wrist, sticky side out.
2. Let the children attach small leaves and flowers to the masking tape to make a nature bracelet.

Adaptation:
* String leaves and flowers on old shoelaces or yarn to make a necklace.

STICKY PICTURE

Skill: creativity; eye/hand coordination

Materials:
* self-stick vinyl (old scraps work well)
* scissors

Directions:
1. Cut the self-stick vinyl so that each child has a small piece.
2. Peel off the back. Then let children apply grass, leaves, flowers, and other small objects to the sticky side.

PET ROCKS

Skill: creativity; eye/hand coordination

Materials:
* rocks
* markers, paints
* wiggly eyes, yarn, and so on
* glue

Directions:
1. Let each child find a rock he or she can hold in his or her hand.
2. After cleaning their rocks, let them decorate the rocks with paints, wiggly eyes, and yarn.
3. Have the children name their pet rocks and make up a story about them.

Adaptations:
* Older children can write directions about caring for pet rocks.
* Pet rocks make a cute gift!
* Put decorated rocks together to make a "rock band."

NATURE RUBBINGS

Skill: creativity

Materials:
* old crayons
* paper
* leaves, flowers, feathers

Directions:
1. Let children collect objects with different textures on the playground.
2. Remove the paper from several crayons.
3. Place paper over the objects, then rub over gently with the side of the crayon.

Adaptations:
* Let the children guess what objects made the different designs on each other's papers.
* Rubbings can also be made on solid pieces of fabric.

NATURE WEAVING

Skill: eye/hand coordination; creativity

Materials:
* styrofoam meat tray or corrugated cardboard (7" × 9")
* yarn, tape, scissors
* feathers, small sticks, straw, and so on

Directions:
1. Cut five notches on two sides of the cardboard.
2. String the yarn through the notches and tape in the back.
3. Let the children find feathers, small sticks, straw, and other items in nature to weave through the yarn in an over/under pattern.

 # DRIED FLOWER DESIGNS

Skill: creativity

Materials:
* small, flat flowers and leaves
* paper towels
* large, heavy books
* heavy paper
* rubber cement

Directions:
1. Arrange flowers and leaves on one paper towel. Place another paper towel on top, then press between two books for several days.
2. Glue flower designs to paper with rubber cement to make note-cards, nametags, or bookmarks.

IRONED FLOWERS

Skill: creativity

Materials:
* wax paper
* small, flat flowers or leaves
* iron
* construction paper

Directions:
1. Ask the children to find several pretty leaves or flowers on the playground.
2. Lay the objects on one sheet of wax paper, then cover with another sheet of wax paper.
3. Press with an iron. (CAUTION: This must be done by an adult only.)
4. Trim the paper or frame with construction paper.

Adaptations:
* This is a fun activity in the fall with pretty autumn leaves or in the spring with pansies.
* You can also iron crayon shavings between the wax paper.

HIKER'S NECKLACE

Skill: creativity

Materials:
* film containers
* hammer and large nail
* plastic cord or string
* stickers, markers
* scissors

Directions:
1. Using the hammer and nail, make a hole in the bottom of the film container and the lid.
2. Cut a piece of cord or string that will fit over the child's head easily, then thread it through the two holes and tie the ends in a knot.
3. Decorate with stickers or markers.
4. Put a bandaid, the child's name and address, and so forth, in the film container.

Adaptations:
* This is a great place for children to keep their money on a field trip.
* A piece of candy, gum, and balloon make this a fun party favor.

Note: This project is not recommended for very young children, as they should not wear necklaces or be given things on which they could choke.

FOOD COLOR DIP

Skill: creativity; color experimentation

Materials:
* food coloring
* paper towels
* four plastic cups
* water

Directions:
1. Fill each cup halfway with water.
2. Add ten drops of food coloring to each cup.
3. Have the children fold a paper towel into a small square.
4. Dip each corner of the square into a different color.
5. Open and dry.

Adaptations:
* Use the paper towel for a placemat.
* Drop food coloring and water mixture on a coffee filter with an eye dropper.

 # COFFEE FILTER CREATIONS

Skill: creativity

Materials:
* coffee filters
* water-soluble markers
* white paper
* spray bottles with water

Directions:
1. Let the children draw designs on the coffee filters with the markers.
2. Lay the coffee filter on the white paper, then spray with the water and watch the colors fade.
3. Put this in the sun and let it dry.
4. Lift the coffee filter and you will see a pretty design on the white paper.
5. Use the coffee filter to make a butterfly, flower, or snowflake.

GRAB BAG ART

Skill: creativity

Materials:
* lunch bag
* glue, scissors
* scrap paper

Directions:
1. Give each child a lunch bag and ask them to take it home and go around their house and collect some "clean" junk. (Discuss various objects that we often throw away, like cardboard dowels and styrofoam meat trays, that could be recycled.)
2. Let the children trade bags when they come to school the next day to see what they can create from the materials in their bags.

Adaptation:
* Ask each child to invent something from the recycled materials.

WORM PAINTING

Skill: creativity

Materials:
* rubber worms
* paint
* paper

Directions:
1. Let the children take the worms and dip them in the paint.
2. Have them "wiggle" the worms across their page to make a design.

Adaptation:
* Give the children yarn, wet noodles, strips of fabric, and other things to dip in paint and dribble across paper.

SIDEWALK ART

Skill:	creativity

Materials:
* colored chalk
* sidewalk
* paper

Directions:
1. Let the children draw with colored chalk on the sidewalk.
2. Place the paper over the drawing and rub to get a design on the paper.

Adaptations:
* Practice writing names or making shapes, letters, and numerals with chalk on the sidewalk.
* Decorate the sidewalk or front of your school for holidays, family socials, and other special activities.
* Have one child stand on the sidewalk, while another child traces around his or her shadow.

Note: Be sure to get the principal's approval before doing any of these chalk/sidewalk activities.

 BUBBLE PAINTING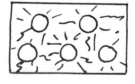

Skill: creativity

Materials:
* 2 or 3 small bottles of bubbles
* food coloring
* large sheets of paper
* clothespins or tape

Directions:
1. Put a large squirt of food coloring in each bottle of bubbles.
2. Attach the paper to the fence with clothespins or tape.
3. Dip the bubble wand in the bubble solution, then blow onto the paper. The bubbles will pop and make a beautiful design.

FROSTED PICTURE

Skill:	creativity
Materials:	* construction paper (dark colors work best) * crayons * Epsom salt * cups, paintbrushes
Directions:	1. Draw a picture with the crayons. Color darkly. 2. Mix ½ cup Epsom salt with ½ cup hot water. 3. Paint the salt and water mixture over the picture. 4. As it dries, crystals will "grow" on the page.
Adaptation:	* This is a good technique for Halloween, space, underwater, or snow pictures.

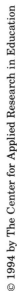

 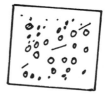

BUBBLE WRAP PAINTING

Skill:	creativity
Materials:	* bubble wrap packing * paints, paintbrushes * paper
Directions:	1. Paint a picture directly on the bubble wrap. (Designs work best.) 2. Place the painting on top of a sheet of paper and rub gently. 3. Lift and see the unusual print you have made.

FRIENDSHIP PAINTING

Skill: cooperation

Materials:
* 2 friends
* cardboard box lid
* paper
* marbles or golf balls
* paint, spoon

Directions:
1. Put a large sheet of paper in the box lid.
2. Drop a golf ball or marble in the paint, then put it on the paper with the spoon. (Two balls and two different colors of paint work best.)
3. Let two children hold opposite ends of the box and cooperate to make a marble painting.

Adaptations:

* Do a surprise painting by putting the marbles or golf balls in a shirt box, adding paint, then putting the lid on. The children will be "surprised" when they open the lid and see their painting.
* For the holidays, make a jingle bell painting. Cut paper to fit inside a cheese ball can. Add jingle bells and paint, then put the lid on and "jingle all the way" as you shake the can and sing the song.

 FOOT PAINTING

Skill: creativity

Materials:
* tempera paint
* 2 pie pans
* butcher paper
* soap, water, towels

Directions:
1. Pour a little tempera in each pie pan.
2. Roll out the butcher paper on the sidewalk.
3. Help one child at a time take off his or her shoes, step in the paint, and walk across the paper.
4. Wash and dry feet. (It's best to do this on a sunny day.)

T-SHIRT DESIGNS

Skill:	creativity

Materials:
* fabric crayons (you can purchase these at most craft stores)
* paper
* old T-shirt
* iron

Directions:
1. Let the children create their own designs for their T-shirts on the paper. For best results press hard with the crayons and fill in spaces. (Words and letters need to be written backwards to print correctly when applied to the shirt.)
2. Place the crayon design next to the T-shirt.
3. Rub over firmly with a hot iron. (CAUTION: This should only be done by an adult.)

Adaptations:
* Let each child decorate a square of white fabric with this technique. (Help them write their name.) Sew the squares together to make a class quilt to hang on the wall. (Solicit the help of a parent to put your quilt together.)
* Make placemats, napkins, doll blankets, and other items for the Housekeeping Center with fabric crayons.
* Decorate curtains for your classroom with fabric crayons.

 **KAZOO**

Skill: creativity; music

Materials:
* toilet paper dowels
* wax paper, rubber bands
* crayons, markers

Directions:
1. Decorate the dowels with markers or crayons.
2. Take a piece of wax paper and cover one end of the dowel using the rubber band to keep it in place.
3. Hum a song into the kazoo.

Adaptations:
* Have a kazoo parade.
* Play "Name That Tune."

SUN CATCHER

Skill:	creativity

Materials:
* laminating scraps
* permanent markers
* hole punch
* yarn

Directions:
1. Cut the laminating film into geometric shapes.
2. Let the children decorate the shapes with markers.
3. Punch a hole and hang with a piece of yarn. You can hang these outside in a tree or inside near a window to catch the sun.

Adaptations:
* Cut holiday shapes, animals, or other objects from the laminating film.
* Make sun catchers from plastic lids.

 LUNCH BAG CITY

Skill: creativity

Materials:
* paper lunch bags
* markers or crayons
* newspaper

Directions:
1. Take one lunch bag, turn it upside down, and draw a picture of a building or a house on it.
2. Take another bag and fill it with newspaper strips.
3. Insert the decorated bag on the stuffed bag to make a building that will stand up.

Adaptations:
* Use these houses and buildings to make a town in the grass or sand. Children can drive little cars and trucks around and play with them.
* When older children study about communities, let them make various buildings, such as the post office, bank, school, and so on.

PLASTER OF SAND

Skill: molding; creativity

Materials:
* 4 cups of sand
* 2 cups of water
* 2 cups of cornstarch
* large pan (use an old one)

Directions:
1. Combine the sand, water, and cornstarch in a large pan.
2. Heat on low, stirring constantly, until the mixture thickens.
3. Set aside and allow to cool.
4. Mold into castles, animals, and other shapes. Allow to dry.

Adaptations:
* You can tint the mixture with liquid tempera if you desire.
* Decorate with small shells and other natural objects. (This makes a nice paperweight or gift.)

 SAND PAINTING

Skill: painting; creativity

Materials:
* sand
* dry tempera
* cups and spoons
* glue
* paper

Directions:
1. Mix sand and dry tempera in the cups with a spoon.
2. Make a design or picture on the paper with the glue.
3. Sprinkle colored sand over the glue, then shake off the excess.

 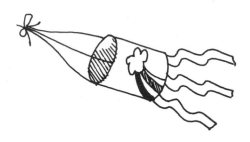

WIND SOCK

Skill: creativity

Materials:
* 24" × 12" or 18" × 8" piece of construction paper or posterboard
* crayons, markers, or paint
* tissue paper
* string or yarn
* hole punch, scissors, glue

Directions:

1. Place the paper lengthwise and draw a picture or paint a design.
2. Cut strips of tissue paper approximately 1" × 18" long.
3. Turn the paper over, then glue the tissue strips to the bottom edge.
4. Curve the sides around to make a cylinder and glue or staple.
5. Punch three holes in the top that are spaced apart evenly.
6. Take three 18" pieces of yarn and tie one end of each in a hole. Bring the other ends together and knot at the top.
7. Hang wind socks from the ceiling or a tree.

Adaptations:
* Let the children make a wind sock of a favorite book, about themselves, or to relate to a unit of study.
* "Baby" wind socks can be made with toilet paper dowels. Decorate the dowel with markers or crayons, glue ½" × 10" strips of tissue paper to the bottom, then punch holes and attach yarn to the top.

FLAGS AND PENNANTS

Skill: creativity

Materials:
* construction paper, cardboard, or solid fabric
* markers, crayons, or paints
* scissors

Directions:
1. Let the children cut out pennants or flags and decorate with markers, crayons, or paint.
2. Hang on the playground.

Adaptations:
* Let the children make flags of different states or countries.
* Staple flags and pennants to a plastic straw or tape to the cardboard dowel from a pants hanger.

 # SIT UPON

Skill: weaving; creativity

Materials:
* 6 sheets of newspaper
* scissors

Directions:
1. Cut the newspapers in half along the middle fold line.
2. Take 11 sheets and fold them into 2" strips.
3. Lay out six strips on the ground in front of you lengthwise.
4. Weave the other five strips through these in the opposite direction.
5. Roll and tuck ends under woven strips.
6. Sit upon these for sing alongs, snacks, stories, and so forth.

Adaptation:
* Cut grocery bags into 12" squares, punch holes around the edges, then sew three sides together with yarn. Stuff with newspaper, then sew up the fourth side.

SUN PRINTS

Skill: creativity

Materials:
* purple or blue construction paper
* a sunny summer day (no wind)

Directions:
1. Take the children out on the playground early in the day.
2. Have the children find a rock and several other interesting items found in nature.
3. Give each child a piece of paper and have them arrange their objects on the paper in a place where the paper will receive direct sunlight most of the day. (The rock should keep the paper from blowing away.)
4. Before the children go home, let them check their papers to see how the sun has "made" a picture for them. "What happened where you put things? Why? What other things does the sun make fade?"

Adaptations:
* Play a guessing game about which objects made the different prints on their paper.
* Let the children do shadow drawings by drawing around the shadows of various objects on large sheets of paper or on the sidewalk with chalk.

WHEELS OF ART

Skill: creativity

Materials:
* small toy cars and trucks
* large sheets of paper
* paint, paper plates

Directions:
1. Pour a small amount of paint in the paper plates.
2. Let the children take a car, dip the wheels in paint, and "drive" it across their paper.

Adaptation:
* Tape a marker to a small car and let the children use it to make designs on a sheet of paper.

RAINBOW WAND

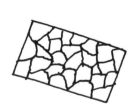

Skill: creativity

Materials:
* paper plates
* tissue paper
* crayons or markers
* scissors
* stapler

Directions:
1. Cut a paper plate in half, then cut off the rim as shown to resemble a rainbow.
2. Color the rainbow with markers or crayons.
3. Cut the tissue paper into 1" strips that are 2 to 3 feet long.
4. Staple four or five strips of tissue paper to one end of the rainbow.
5. Let the children run around with their rainbow wands or make up a dance to music with them.

Adaptation:
* Staple tissue paper to a plastic drinking straw to make a dancing wand.

 TISSUE PAPER FADE

Skill: creativity

Materials:
* tissue paper (at least 3 colors)
* white paper
* mister or spray bottle with water

Directions:
1. Let the children cut or tear the tissue paper into 1" or 2" pieces.
2. Have the children arrange the tissue paper on the white paper.
3. Spray the paper with water, then set it in the sun to dry.
4. Peel off the tissue paper and see the pretty design that it made when it faded.

 ROCK GARDEN

Skill: creativity

Materials:
* small rocks or pebbles
* glue
* heavy paper or cardboard
* crayons or markers

Directions:
1. Take the children on a nature walk and let them each find a small rock.
2. Have the children glue the rock to their paper.
3. Encourage the children to draw a picture around the rock, incorporating it in their picture.

Adaptation:
* Use sea shells or leaves in a similar manner.

 NEGATIVE SPACE

Skill: creativity

Materials:
* paper
* paint, markers, or crayons
* scissors

Directions:

1. Cut a hole in each piece of paper. (It can be any shape.)
2. Give each child a paper with a hole and ask them to draw a picture.
3. Children will really be challenged to think of how they can incorporate the negative space into their picture.

PICK-UP-AND-GO ART

Skill: creativity

Materials:
* detergent box with a handle
* scissors, hole punch, paper, markers, crayons, tape, glue, wallpaper scraps, lunch bags, paper plates, toilet paper dowels, buttons, or yarn

Directions:
1. Let the children decorate the outside of the box any way they would like.
2. Fill the box with some of the materials suggested above. (Rotate materials to keep children interested.)
3. Let the children take the box any place in the classroom or outside to create something from the materials in the box.

Adaptation:
* Children may enjoy taking the art box home with them to make things.

© 1994 by The Center for Applied Research in Education

ART PARADE

Skill: self-esteem

Materials:
* paintings, collages, and other art projects
* record player and record

Directions:
1. After the children have completed an art project, let them get their picture, hold it in front of them, and march around the room to music.
2. They'll be proud and you'll have time to clean up or prepare for the next activity.

Water, Sand, and Block Play

Mud pies, rainbow rice, a bubble machine, icicle sun catcher, and more await the senses as you splash around and make a mess. Props for block play and construction ideas are also presented.

BUBBLE MACHINE

Skill: observing; questioning

Materials:
* margarine tub with lid
* straw
* hole punch
* commercial or homemade bubble mixture

Directions:

1. Punch two holes in the lid of the margarine tub as shown.
2. Place a small amount of the bubble mixture in the tub, then put on the lid.
3. Stick a straw in one of the holes and blow.
4. Observe what comes out of the other hole.
5. "Where did the bubbles come from?" "What made the bubbles?" "What makes bubbles pop?"

Adaptations:

* You can make individual bubble cups for the children in your room with this simple method. Put a small amount of water, a squirt of detergent, and a drop of food coloring in a paper cup. Give the child a straw and let them "blow" for it!

* Make water play day more fun with body bubble painting. Let the children stir up bubbles in a pan with an egg beater. (Put a little water, detergent, and food coloring in the pan to make the bubbles.) "Paint" your body by applying the bubbles to your arms, legs, chin, and so on. (Take a mirror outside so the children can see how silly they look.) Rinse in a sprinkler or with a plastic spray bottle.

 GIANT BUBBLES

Skill: sensory stimulation

Materials:
* 1 cup Joy™ or Dawn™ detergent
* ¼ cup glycerine
* 10 cups water

Directions:
1. Mix the ingredients in a large pan.
2. Allow the mixture to sit at room temperature for one hour.
3. Blow bubbles with fly swatters, plastic rings from drink cans, berry baskets, coat hangers stretched into desired shapes, and so forth.
4. Store the bubble mixture in a covered container in the refrigerator.

 KARO® BUBBLES

Skill: sensory stimulation

Materials:
* 2 cups Joy™ detergent
* 6 cups water
* ¾ cup white Karo® corn syrup

Directions:
1. Combine the ingredients and let sit at room temperature.
2. Blow bubbles.
3. Store the mixture covered in the refrigerator.

Adaptation:
* Make individual bubble wands for the children from pipe cleaners.

169

 **BOB ALONG**

Skill: experimenting

Materials:
* ping-pong balls
* permanent markers
* tub of water

Directions:
1. Draw faces on the ping-pong balls with markers.
2. Let the children experiment with the balls in a tub of water or at the water table.

Adaptation:
* Children can write "secret messages" on small pieces of paper, put them in film containers, and float them in the water table.

© 1994 by The Center for Applied Research in Education

ICEBERGS

Skill: sensory stimulation

Materials:
* plastic bowls
* water, freezer
* water table

Directions:
1. Fill several large plastic bowls with water and put in the freezer.
2. Put these blocks of ice in the water table and allow the children to observe them and play with them.

Adaptations:

* Add plastic polar bears, seals, walruses, and other arctic animals for the children to play with on the ice.
* Put a few drops of food coloring in the water before you freeze it.
* Add ice cubes to your water table outside on a warm day.

170

WATER PAINTING

Skill: sensory stimulation

Materials:
* plastic pails, butter tubs, etc.
* inexpensive paintbrushes

Directions:
1. Give the children a plastic container with water. Let them "paint" the building, playground equipment, fence, or sidewalk.
2. Let them "paint" trees, bushes, and the building with a spray bottle filled with water.

 # RUB A DUB DUB

Skill: sensory stimulation

Materials:
* tubs of water
* mild detergent
* spring clothespins
* doll clothes, handkerchiefs, washcloths, rags

Directions:
1. Let the children wash the doll clothes.
2. Have them hang the clothes on the fence or on a small clothesline to dry.

Adaptations:
* Bring out classroom chairs, plastic toys, dishes, baby dolls, and other items for the children to wash on the playground.
* Older children may enjoy washing the school van.

SINK AND FLOAT

Skill: experimenting; predicting

Materials:
* tub of water
* variety of objects that sink and float (toys, rocks, leaves, corks, coins, pencils, nuts, nails)

Directions:
1. Have the children take objects one at a time and predict if they will sink or float.
2. Tell them to put the objects in the water to see what happens.
3. Group the objects that sink or float together and ask the children how the items are alike.

  COLORED WATER

Skill: experimenting

Materials:
* eye droppers
* food coloring
* clear cups or ice cube trays

Directions:
1. Let the children make primary colors by adding red, yellow, and blue food coloring to three different cups of water.
2. Let them experiment and make secondary colors by using the eye dropper to mix the red, yellow, and blue water in cups or ice cube trays.

Adaptation:
* Surprise the children by adding food coloring to the water in the water table.

 **BOATS**

Skill:	experimenting
Materials:	* toilet paper dowels
	* craft sticks
	* construction paper
	* glue, stapler or tape
	* water table or pan of water

Directions:

1. Staple two toilet paper dowels together.
2. Cut a triangle from the paper and glue to the craft stick to make a sail.
3. Insert the craft stick between the dowels and glue in place.
4. Put the boat in water and watch it sail.

Adaptations:

* Mold a boat from aluminum foil.
* Carve a boat from a bar of Ivory™ soap. Glue paper to a toothpick and insert it in the soap to make a sail.
* You can also make a raft from craft sticks. Lay down two sticks, then glue ten sticks on top of them. Allow to dry, then decorate with permanent markers.

  **SQUIRT! SQUIRT!**

Skill:	eye/hand coordination
Materials:	* plastic spray bottles
	* cardboard dowels or small plastic toys

Directions:

1. Set up the cardboard dowels or toys on a table or fence.
2. Let the children knock them over by squirting them with the water.

Adaptation:

* Use squirt bottles to water plants or the garden.

LETTERS IN THE SAND

Skill:	writing
Materials:	* sandbox
Directions:	1. Smooth out the sand with the palm of your hand.
	2. Draw shapes, letters, and numerals in the sand.
Adaptation:	* Draw pictures with a stick on smooth sand.
	* Use this activity with older children to help them learn spelling words or sight words.

  SAND TRACKS

Skill:	visual matching
Materials:	* cardboard scraps (12" × 6" strips)
	* scissors
	* sand
Directions:	1. On the bottom of the cardboard cut curves, jagged lines, and other designs as shown.
	2. Smooth out the sand with the flat end of the cardboard.
	3. Make tracks in the sand with the cut edge of the cardboard.
	4. Match the tracks with the designs they make.

174

FOOTPRINTS IN THE SAND

Skill: sensory stimulation

Materials: * damp sand

Directions:
1. Let the children take off their shoes and make footprints in the sand.
2. Compare how their footprints are alike and different.

Adaptations:
* Make handprints in the sand.
* Use cookie cutters, plastic toys, and other objects to make prints and molds in the sand.

FUNNEL FUN

Skill: sensory stimulation

Materials: * plastic bottles (milk jugs, detergent, and so on)

Directions:
1. Cut the tops off the bottles.
2. Use them as funnels for water or sand.

Adaptations:

* Poke holes in the bottoms of the plastic containers with an ice pick or hammer. Let the children fill them with sand or water and watch the substance "sprinkle" out.
* Make different sizes of holes in two containers. Ask the children to "estimate" which one will empty first. Why?

SAND SURPRISES

Skill:	small motor
Materials:	* shells
	* bones (cooked and cleaned)
Directions:	1. Hide shells in the sandbox for a surprise.
	2. Let the children pretend they are paleontologists and hunt for bones you have hidden in the sandbox.
Adaptations:	* Put paper clips in the sand, and have children use a magnet to get them out.
	* Hide plastic toys or other objects to go along with a unit of study. For example, you could hide plastic farm animals if you're doing a farm unit, plastic bears for a bear unit, and so on.

TUBS OF FUN

Skill:	sensory stimulation
Materials:	* plastic tubs or water table
	* birdseed
Directions:	1. Fill a tub or water table with birdseed.
	2. Let the children play, measure, and experiment with the birdseed.
	3. The birds will love anything the children spill!
Adaptations:	* Put dry beans, macaroni, cornmeal, cotton balls, and other sensory objects in tubs.
	* Rainbow rice is fun to make. You will need four bags of rice. Color each bag a different color by shaking in a plastic bag with several tablespoons of rubbing alcohol and food coloring. Allow to dry, then mix the different colors together.
	* Mix two different textures for a sensory experience, such as grits and golf tees, styrofoam peanuts and toilet paper dowels, rice and golf balls, and so forth.

ROCK 'N WASH

Skill: sensory stimulation

Materials:
* rocks
* soap and water
* scrub brushes
* pans

Directions:
1. Ask the children to be "rock hounds" and find some rocks on the playground.
2. Fill pans with water and soap and let the children scrub their rocks.
3. Rinse and dry rocks.

Adaptation:
* Ask the children to sort the rocks, count the rocks, seriate the rocks by size, or look at the rocks with a magnifying glass.

PANNING FOR GOLD

Skill: sensory stimulation

Materials:
* gold spray paint
* rocks, pebbles

Directions:
1. Spray the rocks and pebbles gold. (CAUTION: Be sure this is done only by an adult, away from the children.)
2. Hide the "gold nuggets" in the sandbox and let the children use their fingers or toes to find them.

Adaptation:
* Have the children find a "pot of gold" on the playground for St. Patrick's Day.

177

MUD PIES

Skill: sensory stimulation

Materials:
* plastic tub
* shovels, spoons, pails, pans
* dirt, water
* aprons or smocks

Directions:
1. Let the children dig up dirt from a designated area on your playground and fill the plastic tub.
2. Add water and mix well with your hands to make a thick consistency. (If you add too much water, it will be gooey and you'll have to add more dirt.)
3. Make mud pies, cakes, cookies, and other "delicacies," then set in the sun to dry.

Adaptations:

* Making mud pies is an experience that all children need and deserve. Have them wear smocks to minimize the mess or tell parents ahead to dress them in old clothes.
* Put mud in self-locking plastic bags and let the children squish it and play with it.

WINDOW PAINTING

Skill: sensory stimulation

Materials:
* shaving cream
* hose or plastic squirt bottle of water

Directions:
1. Squirt shaving cream on low windows.
2. Let children fingerpaint on the windows.
3. Hose the windows off and you'll have clean windows.

Adaptations:
* Let the children decorate the windows for various holidays with tempera paint to which you add a squirt of liquid detergent. (Clean by fingerpainting with the shaving cream.)
* You can also fingerpaint outside on plexiglass, then hose clean.

SAND AND WATER TOYS

Whether inside or out, vary the toys in the sand and water tables with these materials to give the children new sensory experiences and problem-solving opportunities.

SAND TOYS

cars and trucks
toy dishes and pans
detergent scoops
plastic bottles
plastic farm animals
zoo animals
action characters
blocks
muffin tins, pie pans
plastic spoons
pails and shovels
funnels
shells
salt and pepper shakers
film containers
sifter
shoeboxes

WATER TOYS

sponges
funnels
plastic dishes
plastic toys
boats
tubes
basters and eye droppers
shells
baby dolls
wash cloths, soap, towels
ice cubes
squirt bottles
plastic bottles and containers
tea set
watering cans
film containers
rubber balls

SNOW IS SO MUCH FUN!

If you live in an area where the weather freezes and white flakes cover the ground, bundle the children up and try some of these activities.

* Tint water with food coloring, then paint with brushes on the snow.

* Fill spray bottles with food coloring and water and squirt on the snow.

* Bring snow inside to use in your water table.

* Take out pans, pails, and other containers in which to mold snow.

* Follow each other's footprints in the snow, or make a trail with a stick for children to follow.

* Put an outdoor thermometer on the playground for children to observe the rise and fall in the temperature.

* Make sleds out of cardboard (cut up boxes), pizza pans, plastic lunch trays, and other objects.

* Set up a birdfeeding station for feathered friends. Count the birds that visit your playground.

* Wash doll clothes, then hang them in the freezing weather. What happens? Bring them inside and observe what happens.

* Fill pails and other containers with colored water, freeze, then set on the playground and observe them as they melt.

* Play "Follow the Leader" on the playground.

* Make snow angels by lying on the ground and moving your arms and legs.

* Make forts, houses, furniture, and other things with snow.

* Make snowmen, snowwomen, snowbabies, snowcowboys, and so on, and dress appropriately.

* Make an icicle sun catcher for your playground. Take a pie pan and fill it with water. Add some birdseed, leaves, or small sticks and place the end of a piece of string in it. Freeze, then hang from a tree and watch it sparkle and twirl around.

© 1994 by The Center for Applied Research in Education

BLOCK PROPS

Add interest, challenge, and fun to your Block Center with some of these props:

wooden cars and trucks
street signs
wooden dollhouse
furniture
dolls
stuffed animals
puppets
wooden barn and fence
farm animals
dinosaurs
zoo animals
homemade signs
photographs and pictures of buildings
shoeboxes
milk cartons
wagon
construction hats
boats, airplanes
paper and pencil to make labels for children's buildings
hollow blocks
Lincoln Logs™
Bristle Blocks™

* Ask the children to make letters, numerals, and shapes with blocks.

* Make block patterns for the children to reproduce.

* Have an idea box with pictures of different things the children can build, such as a hospital, park, bridge, house, school, road, or fire station.

* Integrate blocks with a book or unit of study. For example, put three bears and Goldilocks (doll) in the Block Center and ask the children to build their house. Have them build a bridge for the three billy goats gruff, a house for the three little pigs, and so on.

BLUEPRINTS

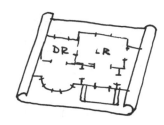

Skill: small-motor movements

Materials:
* blueprints (any builder or architect will give you old ones)
* paper, pencil, tape measure

Directions:

1. Let the children look at blueprints and pretend to build what they see.
2. Add paper, pencil, and tape measure so they can write dimensions, make supply lists, and so forth.

Adaptation:
* Add a carpenter's apron or hard hat for children to wear.

 # MANY KINDS OF HOMES

Skill: small-motor movements; multicultural awareness

Materials:
* pictures of many different kinds of homes (mobile homes, condominiums, apartments, homes from different parts of the world)

Directions:
1. Display pictures of different kinds of homes in the Block Center.
2. Encourage children to try to build different types of dwellings.

Adaptations:
* Add multicultural dolls to the Block Center.
* Provide children with grass, rocks, sticks, and other kinds of building materials.

CARDBOARD CONSTRUCTION

Skill: small-motor movements; creativity

Materials:
* cardboard food boxes (cereal, crackers, cookies, and so forth)
* corrugated cardboard boxes
* masking tape

Directions:
1. Have the children save food boxes for several days and bring them to school.
2. Let the children construct forts, castles, rocket ships, and other structures with the boxes and masking tape.

Adaptations:
* Build things to go along with a unit or theme. Paint cardboard constructions.
* Have older children construct things for younger children to play with.
* Let different groups design and make a cardboard construction for the playground.

 # ENVIRONMENTAL SIGNS

Skill: reading

Materials:
* bags from stores and fast-food restaurants
* heavy paper
* scissors, glue
* large craft sticks or paint sticks
* clay

Directions:

1. Cut out logos from bags and glue them to heavy paper.
2. Tape the signs to the sticks and stand them up in the clay.
3. Let the children use them as labels on block structures or make roads with tape on the floor and use them for signs.

Adaptation:
* Use signs with toy cars in the sand table or sandbox.

CARDBOARD BOX BLOCKS

Skill: small-motor movements

Materials:
* detergent boxes or other sturdy boxes
* newspaper
* self-stick vinyl

Directions:
1. Have the children tear newspaper into strips.
2. Stuff newspaper into the boxes.
3. Cover with self-stick vinyl.

Adaptations:
* Giant boxes can be made from empty diaper boxes.
* These boxes can be stored in large garbage bags for easy carrying and storage.
* If self-stick vinyl is too expensive, just tape the box closed. The children really don't care what the blocks look like—they just have fun building with them!

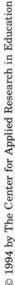

 # NEWSPAPER LOGS

Skill: small-motor movements

Materials:
* newspapers
* masking tape

Directions:
1. Take one or two sheets of newspaper at a time, roll them up, then tape the ends in place.
2. Use newspaper logs to make houses and other play structures by taping them together.

Adaptation:
* You may roll the papers lengthwise or widthwise to make different sizes.

CONSTRUCTION

Woodworking and construction are wonderful vehicles for teaching children cooperation, planning, motor skills, and self-confidence. As with all materials, children need careful supervision and must be taught how to use the tools safely. Here are some other things with which children can build.

Scrap Lumber: Most lumberyards or building sites will be happy to donate scraps to your school.

Plastic Crates: Plastic milk crates are great fun to stack and build with.

Bales of Hay: Bales of hay or pinestraw can be moved around and climbed on.

Tires: Old tires can be used for construction, and they encourage the use of large motor skills. (Only use tires that are *not* steel belted. These have little bits of metal in them that can be dangerous.)

Bricks: Discarded bricks are fun to stack or can be used to make outlines for houses and roads.

Drink Crates: Wooden drink crates can be used for stacking and building.

Spools: Electric companies and phone companies will often donate old wooden spools.

Boxes: Cardboard boxes are super for building houses, trains, animal cages, and space ships.

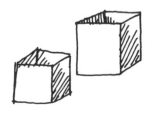

SECTION 6

Dramatic Play

A dramatic play area can be so much more than a sink and stove. With a little imagination and a few props, you can turn it into a grocery store, pet shop, post office, circus, hospital, or anything else you want it to be. Children will also be enthusiastic about using some of these dramatic play props on the playground.

 **CLUBHOUSE**

Skill: social; imagination

Materials:
- ✳ appliance box
- ✳ utility knife
- ✳ paints and brushes

Directions:
1. Encourage children to help you design where windows and door will be. (CAUTION: An adult must do this.)
2. Let the children paint and decorate the clubhouse.
3. Put pillows or towels, books, and stuffed animals inside the box.

Adaptations:
- ✳ Tree branches stuck in the top of the box will make it look like a treehouse.
- ✳ You can also make a puppet theater out of an appliance box.
- ✳ How about a drive-in restaurant, boat, or hot dog stand?
- ✳ Have the children help you think of other things you can create out of large boxes.

 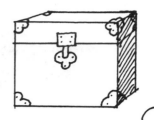

DRESS-UP TRUNK

Skill: social; imagination

Materials:
- large box
- dress-up clothes (men's, ladies', children's)
- shoes, bags, hats, pocketbooks
- jewelry, scarves, gloves, glasses, and so on

Directions:
1. Decorate the box to look like a trunk.
2. Fill with clothes and accessories.

Adaptations:
- Take the trunk outside for the children to play with.
- Let the children use the dress-up clothes for dramatizing stories or putting on skits.
- Ask parents to donate old Halloween costumes to your class.

 AHOY!

Skill: social; imagination

Materials:
- old rowboat

Directions:
1. Prop up the boat in a corner of your playground.
2. Children will enjoy climbing on the boat and using it for dramatic play.

Adaptation:
- Add hats, swim rings, fishing poles, and other props.

 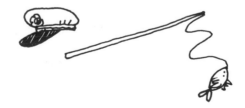

 **PHONE BOOTH**

Skill: social; oral language

Materials:
* large appliance box
* yarn, masking tape
* 2 paper cups, toilet paper dowel
* notepad and pencil
* X-acto™ knife

Directions:
1. Cut a door and two windows in the box with the X-acto™ knife. (CAUTION: An adult must do this.)
2. Make a third window by cutting along the top and two sides. Bend in half, then bend down as shown to make a shelf. Tape in place.
3. To make a telephone, tape the paper cups to the toilet paper dowel. Tie one end of a 2-foot piece of yarn to the toilet paper dowel and tape the other end to the shelf in the box.
4. Place the notepad and pencil on the shelf and let the children make phone calls and take messages.

Adaptation:
* The children will enjoy painting or decorating the box with markers and crayons. The phone booth is a perfect prop for a restaurant, a filling station, store, and so on.

 TABLE AND STOOLS

Skill: dramatic play

Materials:
* spools from a cable company or electric company

Directions:
1. Use a large spool as a table, and smaller spools as seats.
2. Let the children paint and decorate the spools with markers or paint.

Adaptation:
* Use for snacks, art, or a writing table on the playground.

 **POST OFFICE**

Skill:	social; writing
Materials:	* junk mail
	* cardboard box
	* grocery bag
	* paper scraps, pens, pencils

Directions:
1. Cut the top half off the grocery bag. Cut a strip from the piece you cut off and staple to the bag to make a strap.
2. Cut a 6" × 2" slot in one side of the box.
3. Let the children drop the junk mail in the slot or write their own letters and cards to each other.
4. The "mail carrier" can put the mail in the bag and deliver it to all his or her friends.

Adaptation:
* Have the children ride a tricycle or use a wagon when delivering the mail.

  GO FISHING

Skill:	social; imagination
Materials:	* egg carton
	* pipe cleaner
	* stick
	* string

Directions:
1. Cut the egg carton in half.
2. Attach a pipe cleaner to the top to make a tackle box.

3. Tie a piece of string on the stick to make a fishing pole.

Adaptations:
* Tie a sponge fish or other small water animal to the end of the line.
* For younger children, tie a 12" piece of yarn to a straw to make a fishing pole.

CAMP

Skill:	social; imagination
Materials:	* tent, sleeping bags, backpacks
	* mess kit, canteens, flashlight
	* rock and sticks for pretend fire
	* old clothes
Directions:	1. Let the children set up "camp" and build a pretend fire.
	2. Allow them to dress up, play with the backpacks and mess kit, and so forth.
	3. Serve snacks in the camping area.

CAR WASH

Skill:	social; large-motor movements
Materials:	* large box
	* garbage bag
	* tape
	* X-acto™ knife
Directions:	1. Cut a large tunnel out of two sides of the box as shown. (CAUTION: An adult must do this.)
	2. Cut the garbage bag into 1″ strips.
	3. Tape the strips to the inside of the tunnel so they hang down about halfway in the "entrance" and "exit."
	4. Let the children paint the outside of the box or decorate it with crayons.
	5. Children can drive their tricycles and riding toys through the car wash.

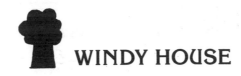 

WINDY HOUSE

Skill: social; imagination

Materials:
* kitchen furniture, table, and chairs
* dolls, beds, strollers
* dishes, phone, cloth bags, dress-up clothes

Directions:

1. Move housekeeping equipment out onto the playground to a cozy spot.
2. Call it the "windy house" because the wind can blow through it.
3. Give children props and dress-up clothes for dramatic play.

DOLLS

Skill: social

Materials:
* flannel cut into 16" to 30" squares
* poly fiberfill
* yarn or thin ribbon

Directions:

1. Ball up the fiberfill and place it in the middle of the square.

2. Wrap the fabric tightly around it to make a head and tie securely with yarn or ribbon.
3. Take two ends, stretch them out to make arms, then tie off at the ends to make hands.

Adaptations:

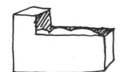

* For young children, you can decorate the dolls with fabric markers. Buttons, yarn hair, wiggly eyes, and other features can be sewn on for older children.
* Make beds for the dolls from cardboard boxes.
* Tie their arms to a tree and swing them.

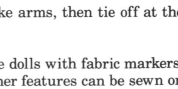

DRAMATIC PLAY KITS

A convenient way to store materials for different themes is to create dramatic play kits. Let every teacher in the school select a different theme, then collect materials to decorate a box. Store these boxes in a central closet so everyone can share in the fun.

Gas Station:

gas pump (cardboard box with portion of old hose attached); spray bottles; rags; old shirts; play money and credit cards (cut up styrofoam meat trays); cash register (shoebox or detergent box); play phone; tools; maps; flashlight; auto parts catalog; funnel; riding toys

Doctor's Office:

bandaids; cotton balls; eye dropper; cotton swabs; notepad and pencil; appointment book; phone; empty medicine bottles; tongue depressor; eye chart; scrub suit; white smock; dolls; blankets; stethoscope; nurse's hat; outside, a wagon for an ambulance

Restaurant:

table and chairs; carry-out bags; cups; napkins; silverware; plastic dishes; tray; pad and pencil; menu; cash register and play money; play phone; apron; chef's hat; pictures of food glued to paper plates; riding toys for a drive-in

Beauty Parlor/ Barber Shop:

mirror; rollers; combs and brushes; hats; empty shampoo and hair spray bottles; hair dryer (cut the cord off); hair nets; barrettes; ribbons; appointment book; telephone; magazines; wigs; empty nail polish bottles; empty make-up containers; play money

Flower Shop:

plastic pots; artificial flowers; gloves; pictures; seed packets; seed catalogs; baskets; vases; watering can; play garden tools; notepad and pencil; phone

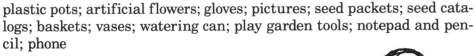

Wedding:

fancy dresses; scarves (for veil); sports jackets; old camera; rings; basket and plastic flowers; tape of "The Wedding March"; rice bags; guest book

Shoe Store:

old shoes (men's, ladies', children's, infants'); phone; cash register; play money; purses; billfolds; socks; mirror; notepad and pencil; shoe shine kit

Our House:

multicultural dolls; baby blankets; books and magazines; placemats; pictures; plastic flowers; ironing board; mirror; bags; native dress from other countries; accessories; ethnic cooking utensils; empty ethnic food boxes; picture window (landscape scene with fabric curtain draped over it)

Birthday Party:

hats; party plates and cups; empty wrapped packages; pretend cake; banner and decorations; party games; party favors

Sports Store: athletic shoes; balls; bats; racquets; goggles; t-shirts; jerseys; hats; pompons; pennants; sports posters; sweat bands; knee pads; sports magazines; cash register and play money; sports equipment

Travel Agency: posters; brochures; world magazines; phone; calendar; suitcases; souvenirs; tickets; maps; dress-up clothes

   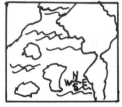

Police: hats; badges (cardboard star wrapped in aluminum foil); notepad (for writing tickets); pencil; whistle; traffic signs; walkie-talkies; "wanted" posters; riding toys

Puppet Show: puppets; puppet theater (made from a large box); play money; cash register; tickets; programs; concession stand; cups; empty candy and popcorn boxes; microphone (stick a ball of black tissue paper in a toilet paper dowel)

Drive-In Bank: play money; box for teller machine; cardboard credit cards; paper and pencils; telephone; calculator; typewriter; play checks; envelopes; riding toys

Picnic: sunglasses; basket; tablecloth; play food; paper products; radio; beach ball; umbrella; beach towels; fishing pole; bathing suits

Pet Shop: stuffed animals; plastic bowls; empty boxes of pet food; pet toys; brush; grooming supplies; cardboard boxes for cages; fish bowl; bird cage; phone; cash register; play money

Bakery: cookie cutters; chef's hats; apron; rolling pin; cake pans; bowls; empty boxes; measuring cups and spoons; towels; play dough; spatula; bags; cash register; play money

Grocery Store: empty food containers; grocery bags; play money; cash register; paper and pencil; apron; purses; billfolds; play food; phone; wagon or grocery cart

Ice Cream Stand: cups; spoons; napkins; paper and pencil; play money; cash register; ice cream cartons; scoops; cardboard cones; bags; aprons; hats; cardboard ice cream scoops

Office: typewriter; cash register; calculator; paper; pencils; computer; coffee cups; calendar; dress-up clothes; file folders; self-stick notes; tape; stapler; paper clips; phone

Circus: costumes; tickets; play money; hula hoops; balls; balance beam; cups; peanut bags; stick horses; face paint; jump rope; stuffed animals

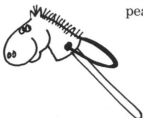   

Train: cardboard boxes; tickets; hole punch; engineer caps; kerchiefs; dress-up clothes; bell

Fire Station: wagon; old hose cut in sections; bell; flashlight; old raincoats; boots; fire helmets; flashlight; airtank made from two plastic liter bottles

School: books; paper; pencils; pens; crayons; markers; safety scissors; hole punch; stapler; tape; chalkboard; chalk; lunchbox; school bag; bell; clock; flag; folders; spiral-ring notebook; grade book; lesson-plan book; glasses; clipboard

Construction: blueprints; safety glasses; paper and pencil; tools; wood scraps; hard hats; work shirts; carpenter's apron; walkie-talkie; lunch box

Craft Store: fabric scraps; wallpaper book; buttons; yarn; felt; glue; safety scissors; markers; crayons; tape; lunch bags; paper plates; wood scraps; trimmings (lace and rickrack); old socks; cash register; paper and pencil

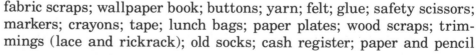    

SECTION 7

Motor Skills and Homemade Equipment

Get those small and large muscles moving with these games and materials. From balls and beanbags, to puzzles and goofy golf, you'll learn how to make it in this section.

SQUISHY BAG

Skill: small-motor movement

Materials:
* heavy self-lock plastic bag
* shaving cream

Directions:
1. Squirt 1 or 2 cups of shaving cream in the bag and zip it up.
2. Let the children squish the bag.

Adaptations:
* Add food coloring to the shaving cream.
* Put fingerpaint, hair setting gel, whipped cream, or other things in plastic bags for children to squeeze.

 COLOR BAGS

Skill: small-motor movement

Materials:
* cornstarch
* sugar
* food coloring
* pan
* heavy self-lock plastic bags

Directions:
1. Mix 1 cup of cornstarch, ⅓ cup of sugar, and 4 cups of water in a pan and cook over medium heat until thick. (CAUTION: This should be done only by an adult.)
2. Remove from the heat, cool, and separate into thirds. Color each third with red, yellow, or blue food coloring.
3. Add 1 tablespoon of every color to a plastic bag and zip up.
4. Children can squish and squeeze the bags and observe how secondary colors are made.

Adaptation:
* For younger children, secure the bags at the top with wide tape.

STAND UP

Skill: small-motor movement; eye/hand coordination

Materials:
* * cardboard egg carton
* * scissors
* * large crayons

Directions:
1. Turn the egg carton upside down. Punch a large hole in the bottom of each section with the scissors.
2. Give the children crayons to put in the holes.

Adaptations:
* * This is a good way to store markers, scissors, pencils, and other classroom materials.
* * Craft sticks can be decorated with markers and then used in the egg carton.

 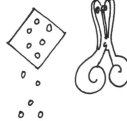

PUNCH IT

Skill: small-motor movement

Materials:
* * paper scraps, wallpaper
* * hole punch

Directions:
1. Give the children paper scraps and let them punch holes.
2. Save the holes they have punched for art projects.

Adaptation:
* * Give children tickets and let them pretend to be train conductors.

SEW AND SEW

Skill: small-motor movement; eye/hand coordination

Materials:
* paper plates or plastic ice cream lids
* hole punch, markers
* shoelaces, yarn, or cord

Directions:
1. Draw a picture on the paper plate or plastic lid with markers.
2. Punch holes around the edges, then let the children sew with shoelaces or yarn.

Adaptations:

* Cut cardboard into shapes or objects that relate to a unit of study, then punch holes around the edges.
* Cut cardboard into large letters or numerals that the children can lace around.
* Use old plastic placemats to make lacing cards. Cut out interesting shapes, then hole punch around the edges.
* Make a lacing card with the child's name from a piece of cardboard.

 STENCILS

Skill: small-motor movement

Materials:
* cardboard or plastic lids
* scissors
* pencils and paper

Directions:
1. Draw simple shapes on the cardboard or plastic lids and cut out.
2. Let the children use these templates to make designs and objects.

Adaptation:
* Give the children jar lids, blocks, and other classroom objects to trace around.

BOX TOP PUZZLES

Skill: small motor

Materials:
* ✳ cardboard food boxes, detergent boxes, and so forth
* ✳ scissors
* ✳ envelope or plastic bag

Directions:
1. Cut off the front of the box.
2. On the reverse side, draw a puzzle shape. (Adapt the number of pieces to the age and ability of your children.)
3. Cut along the puzzle lines, then store in an envelope or plastic bag.

Adaptations:

* ✳ If you have two of the same box, then cut up one and use the other as a pattern for children to look at.
* ✳ Cut boxes in half, fourths, and so on, and let the children put them together as an introduction to fractions.
* ✳ Glue magazine pictures or photographs of children to cardboard, then cut them up to make puzzles.

FLOOR PUZZLE

Skill: small-motor movement

Materials:
* ✳ large pieces of cardboard or paper
* ✳ markers, scissors

Directions:
1. Let the children work together to draw a large mural or picture on the cardboard.
2. Cut the mural into puzzle pieces, then let the children put it together on the floor.

Adaptation:
* ✳ Trace around children's bodies on large sheets of paper. After coloring in on the paper, cut up the shapes to make a large "body puzzle."

BAKER'S DOZEN PLAY DOUGH

Skill: small-motor movement

Materials:
* 2 cups all-purpose flour
* 1 cup salt
* 2 tablespoons cream of tarter
* 2 tablespoons oil
* 2 cups water
* food coloring

Directions:
1. Mix the dry ingredients together. Add the oil, water, and food coloring and stir until smooth.
2. Cook over medium heat until the mixture thickens and sticks to the spoon. (CAUTION: This should be done by an adult only.)
3. Cool, knead, and keep in an airtight container.

Adaptations:
* A baker's dozen of fun things to do with play dough are:

    Roll it, pat it, squeeze it.

     Cut it with scissors.

     Use cookie cutters.

    Make shapes.

     Make letters.

    Make sets.

     Make fingerprints and handprints in it.

    Use spools, beads, blocks and other items to make impressions in it.

    Mix 2 primary colors of dough to make a secondary color. (For example, give every child a small ball each of yellow and blue and have the children squeeze them together to make green.)

     Play a guessing game. Make something and see who can guess what it is.

    Use plastic knives, forks, and play dishes with it.

     Make things with toothpicks, craft sticks, and play dough.

    Use unsweetened Kool-Aid® to color and add a scent to the dough.

CHOPSTICK PICK UP

Skill: small-motor movement

Materials:
* chopsticks
* small toys, blocks, and other classroom objects

Directions:
1. Give the children chopsticks to practice holding and manipulating.
2. Let the children try to pick up different objects with the chopsticks.

SPOON FULLS

Skill: small-motor movement

Materials:
* birdseed or mixed beans
* spoon, plastic bowl, tray
* egg carton or muffin tin

Directions:
1. Fill the bowl with birdseed or beans and place it on a tray with the muffin tin.
2. Let the children spoon beans and birdseed into the muffin tin.

Adaptations:
* Let the children sort the beans with their fingers into an egg carton.
* Use large spoons to do a relay on the playground. Fill a container with water at one end of the relay and place an empty container at the other end. The children can take turns running with spoonfuls of water and to try to fill up the empty container.

 **BASTER**

Skill:	small-motor movement
Materials:	* kitchen baster * 2 plastic bowls * food coloring
Directions:	1. Fill one bowl half full with water. (Add food coloring if you desire.) 2. Ask the children to move the water to the empty bowl using the baster.
Adaptations:	* Let the children fill small containers with an eye dropper. * Give children a sponge to move water from a full bowl to an empty bowl.

 **TONGS**

Skill:	small-motor movement
Materials:	* kitchen tongs * nuts, rocks, pine cones, or small toys * pie pans
Directions:	1. Let the children practice picking up objects with the tongs. 2. Ask them to move the objects from one pan to the next.
Adaptation:	* Children with more dexterous skills could be given tweezers and smaller objects.

 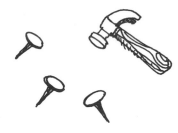

HAMMER, HAMMER

Skill: small-motor movement

Materials:
* golf tees
* plastic hammer
* large piece of styrofoam (used in packaging computers and appliances)

Directions:
1. Let the children take the golf tees and hammer them in the styrofoam.
2. Ask the children to make patterns or designs with the golf tees.

Adaptations:

* Children can also hammer golf tees into the ground outside.
* Hammer nails about halfway in a tree stump, then let the children hammer them in the rest of the way.

STRING ALONG

Skill: small-motor movement; eye/hand coordination

Materials:
* yarn
* dry pasta with holes
* colored straws cut in ½" sections
* scissors, tape

Directions:
1. Cut the yarn in lengths 12" to 24".
2. Wrap a piece of tape around one end of the yarn to make it easier to string. Tie a knot in a straw or piece of pasta at the other end.
3. Let the children string pasta and straws on the yarn.

Adaptations:

* Encourage the children to reproduce a pattern with the pasta and straws.
* Let the children string buttons, old beads, cereal, and other objects with holes.
* Give the children old shoelaces and let them string flowers and leaves outside.

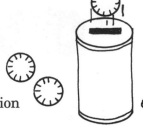

IN THE HOLE

Skill:	small-motor movement; eye/hand coordination
Materials:	* can with plastic lid (potato chip canister, peanuts, coffee, and so forth)
	* poker chips or milk jug lids
	* scissors
Directions:	1. Cut a slit in the plastic lid with scissors. (It should be large enough for a poker chip to slip in easily.)
	2. Give the children the poker chips to put in the hole.
Adaptations:	* Give the children coins to put in a piggy bank.
	* Cut a square hole in the lid of a shoebox or laundry detergent box and let children put in blocks.

 # DRESS ME

Skill:	small-motor movement
Materials:	* old children's clothing
	* teddy bear or other stuffed animal
Directions:	1. Let children put socks, T-shirts, and other clothes on the teddy bear.
	2. Ask the children to dress the bear in mittens, hats, and outdoor clothing.
Adaptation:	* Nail a pair of old tennis shoes to a board so children can practice tying.

POOLS OF FUN

Skill: small-motor movement

Materials:
- * plastic swimming pool
- * stringing beads
- * lacing cards
- * puzzles
- * play dough or clay
- * hole punch, scissors, paper
- * stacking toys, blocks
- * plastic jars and lids

Directions:
1. Put the swimming pool in a quiet area of your room. Each week, fill it with a different manipulative material similar to the ones listed above.
2. Children can get in the pool and play with the toys. This will help contain materials and encourage children to focus on an activity.

Adaptation:
- * Create "pools of fun" for the children on the playground.

HOMEMADE SANDBOX

Skill: sensory stimulation

Materials:
* railroad ties
* tar paper
* sand
* shower curtain, tarp, screen, etc.

Directions:
1. Place the railroad ties in a square shape.
2. Cover the ground with tar paper.
3. Fill with sand.
4. Use an old shower curtain, tarp, or screen as a cover to keep the sand clean.

RICKETY RACKET TENNIS

Skill: coordination

Materials:
* coat hangers
* old panty hose
* cloth tape
* balloons

Directions:
1. Bend the hanger into a diamond shape.
2. Stretch one leg of the panty hose over the hanger and knot it at the end.
3. Bend up the hook on the hanger and tape it to make a handle.
4. Let two children face each other and hit a balloon back and forth with their "rackets."

Adaptation:
* A yarn ball, sponge ball, or masking tape ball can also be used.

 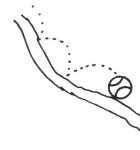

BOUNCY BALL

Skill: large-motor movement; coordination

Materials:
* rubber balls
* chalk

Directions:
1. Draw a path on the sidewalk with chalk.
2. Let the children bounce the ball on the designated path.

Adaptation:
* Older children can draw their own ball paths, making them increasingly difficult.

BALLS OF FUN

Skill: large-motor movement; coordination

Materials:
* little to big balls
* sponge balls, cloth balls, rubber balls, and beach balls

Directions:

1. Throw and catch the balls.
2. Throw the balls at a target or in a basket.
3. Kick them.
4. Kick the balls into a basket or box.
5. Hit the balls with a paddle, bat, or small broom.
6. Roll them on the ground.
7. Sit on them and bounce up and down.
8. Bounce the balls and count how many times you can do it.
9. Throw the ball against a wall, then try to catch it.
10. Hit at the ball with your head, knee, elbow, shoulder, or other parts of your body.
11. Roll the ball down the slide.
12. Play Dodgeball, Kickball, Call Ball, Keep Away, and other ball games.

SCOOP A LOOP

Skill:	coordination
Materials:	* plastic milk jugs * scissors * small balls
Directions:	1. Cut around the milk jug with scissors as shown, leaving the handle and creating a scoop with the top of the jug. 2. Give two children a scoop and have them stand 6 to 10 feet apart from each other. 3. Let the children take turns throwing the ball to each other and trying to catch it in their milk jug.
Adaptation:	* Several children can play this game by standing in a circle and throwing the ball to each other.

HOMEMADE "FRISBEES"

Skill:	large-motor movement; coordination
Materials:	* small, clear plastic lids (from margarine tubs or deli containers) * permanent markers
Directions:	1. Have the children decorate lids with markers. 2. Let the children throw the lids like Frisbees.
Adaptations:	* Set up a target for the children to aim for, such as a box or hula hoop. * Let the children measure how far they can throw their lids.
Note:	The children need to be reminded not to throw these at or near anyone.

BIG MOUTH BOX

Skill: coordination

Materials:
* cardboard box
* markers or paints
* scissors or knife

Directions:
1. Cut the top flaps off the box.
2. On the bottom of the box, cut an 8" circle with the scissors or a knife. (CAUTION: An adult will need to do this.)
3. Draw a clown's face, lion's head, or other character around the circle using the circle as a mouth. Color with markers or paint.
4. Let the children throw beanbags or small balls into the mouth.

Adaptation:
* Older children could make a similar game in which several holes are cut in the box. Assign points for each hole, then add up the points for each player.

 **BEANBAGS**

Skill: large-motor movement

Materials:
* old socks
* beans or birdseed
* needle and thread

Directions:
1. Cut off the toe of the sock.
2. Fill the toe with one cup of beans or birdseed.
3. Stitch the top securely with a needle and thread.

Adaptations:

* For younger children, fill the beanbags with styrofoam packing, newspaper strips, or other materials that won't hurt if they hit someone with them.
* Fill a small nylon sock with ½ cup dried beans. Twist a rubber band around it, then pull the top of the sock over it to make a beanbag.
* Toss the beanbags into a basket or hula hoop.

MASKING TAPE BALL

Skill: coordination

Materials: * newspaper
      * masking tape

Directions: 1. Take two sheets of newspaper and wad them up into a ball.
      2. Tightly wrap masking tape around the newspaper to form a ball.
      3. Play catch with the ball or toss it at a target.

STOCKING BALL

Skill: coordination

Materials: * old panty hose
      * scissors
      * needle and thread

Directions:

      1. Cut one leg off the panty hose from the knee down.
      2. Take the remainder of the panty hose, wad it into a ball, and stuff it down in the toe of the leg you cut off.
      3. Twist the toe, then pull the leg over it. Continue twisting and pulling the leg over it.
      4. Stitch the top of the panty hose together with needle and thread.

TAIL BALL

Skill: coordination

Materials: * old panty hose
      * scissors

Directions: 1. Cut one leg off the panty hose from the knee down.
      2. Take the remainder of the panty hose, wad it into a ball, and stuff it down in the toe of the leg you cut off.
      3. Tie a knot around the toe with the remaining portion of the hose.
      4. Throw it and watch it glide.

214

YARN BALL

Skill: eye/hand coordination

Materials:
* yarn
* strip of cardboard 2" wide
* scissors

Directions:

1. Wrap the yarn around the cardboard 100 to 150 times.
2. Cut a 1" piece of yarn and fold it in half. Thread it under the wrapped yarn, then bring the ends together and tie in a tight knot.
3. Trim loops with a pair of scissors.

Adaptation:
* Yarn balls can be made in many different sizes by varying the width of the cardboard strip and the number of times you wrap the yarn around it.

CATCH BALL

Skill: eye/hand coordination

Materials:
* plastic milk jug
* scissors
* yarn ball, ping-pong ball, or masking tape ball
* 3-foot piece of string

Directions:

1. Cut around the milk jug as shown.
2. Tie one end of the string to the ball and attach the other end to the inside bottom of the jug.
3. Toss the ball in the air and catch it in the milk jug.

FITNESS TRAIL

Skill: large-motor movement

Materials:
* posterboard
* markers
* tape

Directions:
1. Cut posterboard in fourths.
2. Write a different exercise on each card and illustrate. For example:

   5 sit-ups
   10 jumping jacks
   10 windmills
   5 push-ups
   10 arm circles
3. Tape the cards to different locations around your playground.
4. Go through the fitness trail with small groups of children and demonstrate the exercises.
5. Let the children do the fitness trail on their own.

Adaptations:
* Vary the number of stations and difficulty of exercises based on the children's ability.
* Older children can design their own fitness trail and illustrate the cards.

© 1994 by The Center for Applied Research in Education

CAN CATCH

Skill: coordination

Materials:
* tennis ball
* potato chip canister

Directions:
1. Let the children bounce the tennis ball and try to catch it in the can.
2. Give two children cans to hold and let them bounce the ball back and forth and try to catch it.

FIELD HOCKEY

Skill: large-motor movement

Materials:
* small brooms
* laundry basket or box
* plastic ball, sponge ball, or homemade ball

Directions:
1. Let the children take the brooms and practice hitting the ball into the basket or box.
2. Younger children will have fun doing this individually, but older children may want to divide into teams and keep score.

GOOFY GOLF

Skill: large-motor movement; coordination

Materials:
* fried chicken barrels (or ice cream cartons)
* markers, scissors
* construction paper, glue
* child-size golf clubs and plastic golf balls

Directions:

1. Turn the barrel upside down and cut a hole as shown.
2. Decorate the barrel with markers and paper to look like animals.
3. Set the barrels around your playground and let the children practice hitting golf balls into them.

Adaptations:
* The children can also try to hit golf balls into hula hoops placed on the ground on your playground.
* Small brooms can be used instead of golf clubs to hit balls.

RIDING ROUND-UP

Skill: large-motor movement

Materials:
* riding toys (ask each child to bring one from home)
* chalk

Directions:
1. Block off a portion of your parking lot for children to ride in. (Ask parents and teachers to move their vehicles ahead of time and use cones and other barricades.)
2. Let the children draw streets and direction signs with chalk.

Adaptation:
* Make road signs from posterboard for a language experience activity.

Note: This activity must be carefully supervised.

 DRIVING SCHOOL

Skill: large-motor movement

Materials:
* cardboard cut into 2½" × 3½" rectangles
* small picture of each child
* markers, scissors, glue

Directions:
1. Discuss the rules for using the riding toys on the playground.
2. Make a language experience chart of the rules as children dictate them to you.
3. Role-play situations and "safe driving" on the playground.
4. Let each child take a "driving test" and demonstrate how to start, stop, and park the riding toys.
5. Glue pictures of children on the cardboard and then give them markers to decorate their driver's license. (Laminate or cover with clear self-stick vinyl.)

Adaptation:
* Invite a police officer to discuss bicycle safety.

 **WHEELS OF FUN**

Skill: large-motor movement

Materials: ＊ riding toys

Directions:

1. *Parade:* Decorate riding toys with streamers, construction paper flags, and so forth, and have a parade.
2. *Turns List:* Have a "turns list" where children can write their names to sign up and have a turn riding the tricycles. (You might want to take a minute timer outside and set it for 5 or 10 minutes to help children know when their turn is up.)
3. *Parking:* Make a "parking lot" for riding toys.
4. *Car Wash:* Have the children wear bathing suits one day and wash the riding toys.
5. *Obstacle Course:* Make an obstacle course where children have to drive under objects, around things, or follow a chalk line.
6. *Follow the Leader:* Play follow the leader on the tricycles.
7. *Dancing with Trikes:* Play music and let the children make their tricycles "dance" to the music.
8. *Relays:* Make up relay races for the children to have on the riding toys.
9. *Rainy Day Rides:* When the weather is bad, bring the riding toys inside and let the children ride them in the halls.
10. *Parent Pedal Power:* If you have parents in for a program or party, put them on the trikes and let them race. (Everyone will have a good laugh!)

TIRE TRICKS

Skill: large-motor movement

Materials:
* old tires of various sizes (make sure these are not steel belted tires, as they have metal pieces in them that could hurt the children)

Directions:

1. Use the tires to make an obstacle course.
2. Stand the tires up on the ground to make a tunnel the children can crawl through.
3. Let the children create their own games and structures with the tires.

Adaptation:
* Tires can also be used for a sandbox or garden.

BOWLING

Skill: large-motor movement; coordination

Materials:
* 6 to 10 plastic drink bottles (2-liter size)
* rubber ball

Directions:
1. Have the children set up plastic bottles in a triangular shape.
2. One at a time, let each child stand behind a designated line (vary this from 5 feet to 12 feet depending on the age of the child), roll the ball, and try to knock down the bottles.
3. Count to see how many bottles the child has knocked over. Then have him or her set the bottles back up for the next friend. (Older children may want to keep score and add up their total.)

Adaptation:
* Set up cardboard rollers from toilet paper or paper towels for the children to knock down with a ball.

ELASTIC STRETCH

Skill: large-motor movement

Materials:
* elastic cord ½" to 1" wide
* needle and thread
* markers

Directions:
1. Cut elastic into 4-foot to 7-foot lengths according to the size of your children.
2. Sew the ends together securely to make a loop.
3. Let the children color the elastic loops with markers.
4. Use elastic for stretching and bending exercises.
5. Let two children exercise together with elastic loops.

Note: Supervise the children carefully with these loops to ensure no one gets hurt.

TIN CAN STILTS

Skill: large-motor movement; coordination

Materials:
* large juice cans
* 12-foot rope
* can opener

Directions:
1. Remove labels from cans.
2. Punch two holes in the top of each can directly across from each other.
3. Cut two strips of rope approximately 6 feet long. (The length of the rope will vary depending on the size of the child.)
4. Thread each rope through the holes in the can, then bring the ends together at the top and tie into a knot.
5. The children can stand on the cans, hold the ropes in their hands, and walk by slowly lifting the can and their foot.

Adaptation:
* For younger children, use smaller cans such as those from tuna or vegetables.

PARACHUTE PLAY

Skill: coordination; cooperation

Materials:
* old sheet
* ball

Directions:
1. Have the children stand around the sheet holding the ends.
2. Place a ball in the middle of the sheet. Then shake and wave the sheet and watch the ball bounce.
3. Put several balls on the sheet to make "popcorn."

Adaptations:
* The children will enjoy watching a stuffed animal bounce up and down on the sheet.
* Give two children a towel to use as a parachute for bouncing balls or toy animals.

 BEACH BALL FUN

Skill: coordination; large-motor movement

Materials:
* beach ball
* string

Directions:
1. Hang the beach ball from the ceiling or from a tree branch.
2. Give the children a plastic bat or cardboard roller with which to hit.

Adaptations:
* Make a bat by rolling up a sheet of newspaper and taping the ends.
* Tie a soft doll or stuffed animal to a tree branch for the children to push and swing.

TOPSY TURVY TENNIS BALLS

Skill: coordination

Materials:
* old tennis balls (any tennis player will give you their old "dead" balls)
* markers
* beans or small pebbles

Directions:

1. Make a 2" slit in the tennis ball. (CAUTION: An adult will need to do this ahead of time with a knife.)
2. Let the children put dried beans or pebbles through the slit into the ball to make a shaking noise.
3. Decorate the balls with markers.
4. Play catch, bounce, or throw at a target, such as a hanging beach ball or tire swing.

 # BALANCE BEAM

Skill: balance; large-motor movement

Materials:
* 2" × 4" piece of lumber (10' or 12' long)

Directions:

1. With young children, just lay the piece of lumber on the ground and let them walk on it.
2. As their confidence and skill increases, prop up the board with a wooden frame.

Adaptations:
* Place a jump rope on the ground for the children to walk on. Make it into different configurations and see if they can walk forwards and backwards on it.
* Put masking tape on the floor for the children to walk on. Make letters, shapes, and numerals for them to walk around.

 **CANTEEN**

Skill: small-motor movement

Materials:
* 16-ounce clear plastic bottle
* wide masking tape
* old panty hose
* scissors, markers

Directions:
1. Cut one leg off the panty hose. Tie the ends together in a knot to make a loop.
2. Attach the loop to the plastic bottle with tape to make a shoulder strap.
3. Let the children write their names on their canteens and decorate with permanent markers.
4. Fill with water to save you when you're "dying of thirst!"

Note: Remind the children to wear this over their shoulder only and never to put it around their neck.

Group Games

Whether it's sunny, raining, snowing, or sleeting, you'll find great games for all seasons in this section. Active participation, cooperation, and challenge are the key elements for these educational, indoor, and outdoor games. Children will have tons of fun as social skills, motor skills, and learning objectives are reinforced.

KEYS TO SUCCESSFUL GAMES

When introducing games or playing games, keep these suggestions in mind:

1. Be enthusiastic and positive about the game.

2. Be prepared by having all the equipment you need before you begin.

3. Change the games for the level and interests of your children.

4. Individualize games for the children with special needs.

5. Keep the rules few and simple.

6. Briefly explain the game, then walk through it several times. Encourage children to ask questions if they don't understand.

7. Keep it safe. Demonstrate the proper use and care of all equipment.

8. Praise children for their participation.

9. Encourage cooperation, rather than competition.

10. Observe children and adapt the game if necessary.

11. Stop the game while the children are still interested in it so they will want to play another day.

12. Have *Fun!*

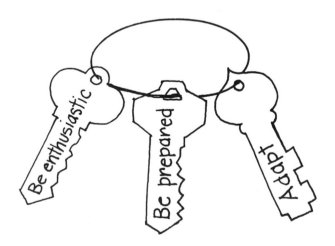

MARVELOUS MACHINE

Skill: large-motor movement

Materials: none

Directions:
1. Choose one child to come to the front of the room to make a noise and motion like a machine. (Bend knees, shake arms, move head from side to side, hum, whirr, ding, and so on.)
2. The first child carries on making his or her motion and sound as another child comes up, stands next to the first child, and makes a different motion and noise.
3. The game continues as each child in the room comes up and adds his or her unique motion and sound to the marvelous machine. Soon the whole room is moving and humming!

THE FREEZE DANCE

Skill: large-motor movement

Materials:
* record and record player

Directions:
1. Put on some music and tell the children to do a silly dance and move around.
2. When you stop the record, tell the children to "freeze" in whatever position they are in.
3. Continue starting and stopping the music as they dance and freeze.

Adaptations:
* Play this game with a partner.
* Put letter or numeral cards on the floor, and when the music stops each child must pick one up and identify it.

FOUR CORNERS

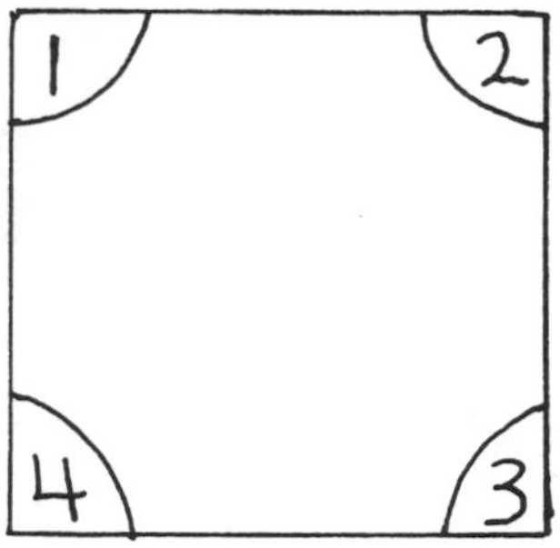

Skill: socialization

Materials: * paper, markers, tape

Directions:

1. Write numerals from 1 through 4 on four sheets of paper. Tape a different numeral in each corner.
2. Choose one person to be "it" and hide his or her eyes. "It" counts slowly to ten as the other children tiptoe to a corner. "It" says "freeze" and calls out the number of one corner. The children who are in that corner are out of the game and must sit in the middle of the room in the "stew pot."
3. "It" begins counting to ten again as the rest of the children tiptoe to a new corner. The game continues until there is one child left who then becomes "it."

ARM DANCING

Skill: large-motor movement

Materials: * record player, record with a slow beat

Directions:

1. Talk about all the movements you can do with your arms. Think of one specific movement you can do in sequential order from one to four. For example: 1—clap your hands; 2—wave your hands in the air; 3—roll them; 4—slap your thighs.
2. Put on the music and dance your hands doing each of the movements above to the count of eight.

Adaptation: * Add more movements as the children become successful.

"A" MY NAME IS

Skill: initial consonant sounds

Materials: none

Directions:
1. Children sit in a circle.
2. The first child completes this chant to the letter "a":

    A—My name is A_____. (Say a name beginning with A.)
    My husband's/wife's name is A_____.
    We come from A_____. (Name a place.)
    And we sell A_____. (Name an object or food.)

3. The second child completes the chant for "b."
4. Continue going around the circle with each child taking a different letter of the alphabet.

Adaptation:
∗ Use this chant as a jump rope rhyme.

 PAPER BALL BATTLE

Skill: large-motor movement

Materials: ∗ scrap paper

Directions:
1. Give each child a scrap sheet of paper and have them wad it up into a ball.
2. Divide the children into two teams and have them face each other 20 to 30 feet apart.
3. When you say "Go," the children begin throwing their paper balls at each other. As soon as a ball lands on your side, pick it up and throw it back at the other team.
4. When you say "Stop," everyone stops. Each team gathers up the balls on its side and counts them.
5. Continue throwing and counting balls.

Adaptation:
∗ Older children may enjoy keeping score.

FOOT SOCCER

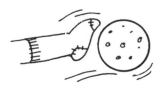

Skill: large-motor movement

Materials: * sponge ball or other soft ball

Directions: 1. Have children sit on the floor in a circle with their legs extended.
                  2. Put the ball in the middle of the circle.
                  3. The children then kick the ball around trying to keep it in the circle.

Adaptation: * Take off your shoes and play "sock soccer."

 # THE QUIET TOUCH

Skill: sequence

Materials: none

Directions: 1. Children may sit in their seats or in a circle on the floor.
                  2. The first child gets up and quietly touches something in the room, then sits down.
                  3. The second child gets up, touches what the first child touched, touches another object, then sits down.
                  4. The third child gets up, touches what the first child touched, touches what the second child touched, then touches another object.
                  5. The game continues with each child touching what previous children have touched in sequential order and adding a new object at the end. The game is over when someone is unable to do this, so you just begin again.

PASS THE PARCEL

Skill: cooperation

Materials:
* small box
* special prize
* tissue paper or newspaper
* tape
* record player

Directions:
1. Put the special prize in the box. (It might be a new book for the classroom, bubbles, colored chalk, stickers, and so on.)
2. Wrap 5 to 10 different layers of tissue paper around the box.
3. Have the children sit in a circle.
4. Begin passing the "parcel" around as you play music.
5. When the music stops, the person holding the package may unwrap one layer.
6. Continue playing the game until the last layer is unwrapped. That person may open up the box and share it with the group.

 **GOSSIP**

Skill: listening

Materials: none

Directions:
1. Have the children sit in a circle on the floor.
2. Whisper a secret message in the first child's ear. (You may only say it one time.)
3. That child passes on the secret to the next person.
4. Keep passing the secret until the last person hears it. The last person then says the message aloud.
5. Compare the original message with the final one!

MOMMA CAT AND KITTENS

Skill: listening

Materials: none

Directions:

1. One child is selected to be momma cat and three others are chosen to be her kittens.
2. Momma cat leaves the room and her kittens hide somewhere in the room.
3. When Momma cat returns, her kittens "meow" and she goes around and finds them.

Adaptation:

* Change this game for different animals and let the children make the appropriate animal sounds (dogs, pigs, snakes, and so on).

 MUFFIN MAN

Skill: socialization

Materials: * blindfold

Directions:

1. One child is blindfolded and stands in the middle of the circle.
2. The other children walk around and sing, "Do You Know the Muffin Man?"
3. You tap one child who walks up to "it." "It" tries to identify who it is by feeling his or her face. That child becomes the next "it."

Adaptation:

* You can play a similar game called "Morning, Judge." One child is blindfolded, and another child comes up, shakes his or her hand, and says in a disguised voice, "Morning, Judge." "It" tries to guess who the child is from his or her voice or handshake.

GOING ON A TRIP

Skill:	auditory memory
Materials:	none
Directions:	1. The children sit in a circle. The first child says, "I'm going on a trip and I'm taking (*names an object*)."
	2. The second child repeats what the first one said and adds a new item.
	3. The game continues until one child forgets the previous items named, and the game starts over.
Adaptations:	* Ask the children to name items in alphabetical order. For example, the first child says something that starts with "a," the second child says something that begins with "b," and so forth.
	* Change the game to pretend you're going shopping. "I'm going shopping and I'm going to buy . . ."

 MISSING

Skill:	listening
Materials:	none
Directions:	1. One child is the mother and one child is chosen to be the police officer.
	2. The mother pretends to cry and says, "Boo hoo, I've lost my child." The police officer says, "What does your child look like?" The mother describes the child's (another student in the class) eyes, hair color, clothing, and so forth.
	3. The police officer walks around the room, picks out the lost child based on the description, and returns the child to the mother.

 **ECHO**

Skill: listening

Materials: none

Directions:
1. You clap out a rhythm or pattern.
2. A child's name is called, and he or she repeats the pattern.

Adaptations:
* Have the children stand up. They can remain standing if they can clap out the pattern, but they must sit down if they can't.
* Play the echo game with a drum or rhythm sticks.

 COPY CAT

Skill: socialization

Materials: none

Directions:
1. Have the children stand in a circle. Choose one child to be the leader.
2. The "leader" shows the rest of the group a silly motion, crazy way to stand, or silly noise to make.
3. When the "leader" calls out "copy cat," the others do their best to mimic the motion and sound.
4. Continue playing the game until everyone has had a turn to be the "leader."

BOOKS UP

Skill: reading

Materials: ✱ reading books or other textbooks

Directions:
1. Ask the children to get out their books and hold them up in the air.
2. After you ask a question, the children use their books to try to find the answer.
3. As the children find the answer, they hold their books up in the air.

 LET'S GO SHOPPING

Skill: oral language

Materials: ✱ toy catalog

Directions:
1. Have the children sit in a circle.
2. One child takes the catalog and opens it up to any page.
3. Another child calls out a number between 1 and 20.
4. The child with the catalog turns the number of pages and tells the group something they'd like on the page.
5. Keep passing the catalog and taking turns.

MIRROR, MIRROR

Skill: large-motor movement

Materials: none

Directions:
1. Divide the class into pairs.
2. One child in each pair is the leader, while the other child is the "mirror" and must do just what the leader does.
3. After several minutes, change roles.

Adaptations:
* Put on some music and let the children mimic each other's dances and motions.
* You can also play this game with the whole group. One person is selected to be "it" and stand in front of the room while the others try to mirror what "it" does.

 **HUMAN CLAY**

Skill: large-motor movement

Materials: none

Directions:
1. Divide the children into pairs.
2. One child is the "sculptor," and the other child is the "human clay."
3. The "sculptor" molds the "human clay" by moving his or her arms, legs, and body all around. The person must try and stay frozen in the position he or she is put in.
4. Let the children trade places after a few minutes.

I SPY!

Skill: visual discrimination

Materials: none

Directions:
1. One child is chosen to be "it."
2. "It" picks an object in the room and says, "I spy something (*names the color of the object*)."
3. The other children take turns guessing what the object is. The first one to guess correctly becomes the next "it."

Adaptations:
* Play "I Spy" by naming beginning sounds of objects. For example, "I spy something that begins with the letter 't.'"
* This is a great game to play looking out the window on a field trip.

WHAT'S DIFFERENT?

Skill: visual memory

Materials: none

Directions:
1. One child is "it" and leaves the classroom.
2. "It" changes one thing on him- or herself, then returns to the room. (The child might unbutton a button, roll up a sleeve, push down a sock, and so forth.)
3. Other children try to guess what's different. The first one to do so becomes the next "it."

MOUSIE, MOUSIE

Skill: socialization

Materials: none

Directions:
1. One child is chosen to be "mousie."
2. Mousie stands in front of the room and says, "Mousie, mousie, how quiet can you be? When I clap my hands one, two, three, we shall see."
3. Mousie claps his or her hands three times, then chooses a friend who is sitting very quietly to come be the next mousie.

LONDON BRIDGE

Skill: socialization

Materials: none

Directions:
1. Pick two children to be the bridge and hold hands to make an arch.
2. Have the other children form a line and walk under the bridge as this song is sung:

> London Bridge is falling down,
> falling down, falling down.
> London Bridge is falling down,
> my fair lady.

3. On the word "lady," the child under the bridge is "captured" and sways back and forth to this verse:

> Take the keys and lock them up,
> lock them up, lock them up.
> Take the keys and lock them up,
> my fair lady.

4. The captured child stands behind one of the children forming the bridge.
5. When all the children have been captured and are standing behind one side of the bridge, the teams lock their arms around each other and have a tug-of-war.

DUCKS IN A ROW

Skill: visual memory

Materials: none

Directions: 1. Five children are chosen to be ducks and line up in the front of the room. The rest of the class looks carefully and tries to remember their order.
2. The ducks leave the room, mix up their order, then walk back in the room.
3. The other children try to remember their original position. The first child to do so correctly gets to choose four friends to be ducks with him or her.

 # PENNY! PENNY!

Skill: socialization

Materials: * penny

Directions: 1. Three children are selected to leave the room.
2. While they are out in the hall, the rest of the children fold their hands on their desk or in their lap. "It" hides a penny in one child's hands.
3. The children in the hall are called back into the room. They go around opening classmates' hands and looking for the penny. The child who finds it first yells "Penny! Penny!" and becomes the next "it."

Adaptation: * Instead of using a penny, hide a small toy that relates to a theme or season, such as a dinosaur, bear, bunny, or pumpkin.

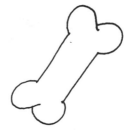

DOGGIE AND BONE

Skill: listening

Materials:
* eraser

Directions:

1. One child is selected to be the Doggie. The Doggie sits with his or her back to the rest of the class and covers his or her eyes. The eraser (bone) is placed behind the Doggie.
2. You tap one child who sneaks up behind the Doggie, barks three times, steals the bone, then returns to his or her seat.
3. The class chants:

   > Doggie, Doggie, where's your bone?
   > Somebody stole it from your home.
   > Guess who? Scooby Doo.

4. The Doggie gets three guesses to identify who stole the bone. If the Doggie doesn't guess correctly, the person who stole the bone becomes the next Doggie.

MUSICAL CHAIRS

Skill: listening

Materials:
* chairs
* record, record player

Directions:

1. Place two rows of chairs back-to-back facing outward. There should be one less chair than the number of people playing this game.
2. When the music starts, all the children march in a circle around the chairs. When the music stops, all the children find a chair and sit down as quickly as they can.
3. The child left standing is out of the game and another chair is removed before the game continues.

Adaptations:

* Vary this game by using carpet squares, paper plates, or construction paper instead of chairs.
* Younger children might enjoy a less competitive version of musical chairs where no chairs are removed. The child who doesn't find a seat just stands out for one round of the game.

SIMON SAYS

Skill: listening

Materials: none

Directions:
1. One person is "it" and faces the rest of the class.
2. "It" calls out various commands that the rest of the group must do if it is preceded by "Simon Says." If they do something that Simon doesn't say to do, then they are out of the game and must sit down.
3. The last child standing becomes the next "it."

HUCKLEBERRY BEANSTALK

Skill: visual discrimination

Materials: * eraser or other small toy

Directions:
1. Choose 4 or 5 children to leave the room.
2. You hide the eraser or toy in plain sight.
3. The children who left the room are called back in and given clues to find the hidden object. "Cold" means they are far away from it, "warm" means they are getting close, and "hot" means they are right next to it.
4. The first one to spot the hidden object yells "huckleberry beanstalk" and becomes the next person to hide the object.

CINDERELLA

Skill: socialization

Materials: * children's shoes

Directions:
1. Have each child remove one shoe and place it in a pile in the middle of the room.
2. Tell the children to close their eyes.
3. You and a helper hide the shoes all around the room in plain sight.
4. You clap your hands twelve times, then the children open their eyes and hunt around the room for their shoe. When they find it, they put it on and return to their seat.

 # BODY TIC-TAC-TOE

Skill: math facts

Materials:
* math flashcards
* red and black construction paper
* scissors
* chalk or tape

Directions:
1. With chalk or tape, draw a large tic-tac-toe frame on the floor. (It needs to be large enough for the children to stand in the spaces.)
2. Cut out 5 large red Xs and 5 black Os from the construction paper.
3. Divide the children into two teams—the Xs and the Os. Give the first five players on the team the Xs and Os.
4. Starting with the Xs, have one child at a time come up and give the answer to a flashcard. If correct, that child may position himself or herself on the tic-tac-toe board any place he or she chooses.
5. The game continues until three players on the same team make a row horizontally, vertically, or diagonally. They can then say, "Tic-tac-toe, three in a row."

Adaptation:
* Use for reinforcing sight words, letters, spelling words, and other information.

 DETECTIVE

Skill: visual memory

Materials: none

Directions:
1. One child is the detective and leaves the room.
2. Another child hides while the detective is out of the room.
3. The detective returns to the room and tries to discover who's missing. The detective gets three guesses, then the missing child becomes the next detective.

Adaptation:
* Let two children trade seats, then see if the detective can figure out who made the "big switch."

 SILLY WILLY

Skill: socialization

Materials: none

Directions:
1. The children stand in a circle.
2. One child is chosen to be Silly Willy.
3. Silly Willy stands in front of one child and tries to make him or her laugh. That child tries to keep a straight face as Silly Willy makes funny faces and says funny things. If the child laughs, he or she trades places with Silly Willy. If he or she doesn't laugh, Silly Willy moves on to someone else.

Adaptation:
* Have one child stand in the middle of the circle while classmates try one at a time to make him or her laugh. Whoever makes the child laugh gets to trade places and stand in the middle of the circle.

HICKLETY PICKLETY BUMBLEBEE

Skill: listening

Materials: none

Directions:

1. Have the children sit in a circle. Start the rhythm of slapping thighs and snapping fingers:

   > slap—snap,
   > slap—snap, and so forth

2. Say this chant to the rhythm as you go around the room using each child's name:

   > Hicklety Picklety
   > Bumblebee.
   > Who can say
   > Their name for me?
   > (*Child's name*).   (Point to a child who
   > (*Repeat name*).   says his or her name.)
   > Clap it,
   > (*Child's name*).   (Say as you clap twice.)
   > Whisper it.
   > (*Child's name*).   (Whisper name.)
   > No sound.
   > (*Mouth child's name with no sound.*)

Adaptation:

* Change this chant to reinforce other skills you are working on. For example, every child could name a zoo animal, color, machine, and so on.

© 1994 by The Center for Applied Research in Education

  # BODY TALK

Skill: listening

Materials: * drum or other musical instrument

Directions:

1. Have the children form a circle. As you play the drum or instrument, tell them to march around.

2. When you stop playing the instrument, call out a part of the body, such as forehead, elbows, knees, and so on. The children must find someone and match up the body part called. For example, if "ankle" is called, they must touch their ankle to someone else's ankle.

Adaptation:

* Let the children take turns playing the instrument and calling out body parts.

AROUND THE WORLD

Skill: sight words

Materials:
* flashcards

Directions:
1. Have the class sit in a circle on the floor or in chairs.
2. One child is "it" and stands behind another child in the circle.
3. You stand in the middle of the circle and show a flashcard to these two children.
4. If "it" replies the correct answer first, he or she then moves and stands behind the next person in the circle. If the child seated responds first, then he or she becomes "it" and trades places with the child standing.
5. The game continues with "it" moving "around the world" (circle). Remember, the same person may make it all around the circle as long as he or she is the first to recognize the words.

Adaptation:
* This game can be used to review math facts, letters, and other information.

BLOCK BUSTERS

Skill: small-motor movement

Materials:
* unit blocks

Directions:
1. Seat the children in a circle and give each one a block.
2. Put one block on the floor in the middle of the circle. Go around the circle and let each child place his or her block on top of the tower.
3. When the tower falls down, begin again.

WIN, LOSE, OR DRAW

Skill: cooperation

Materials:
* index cards
* markers
* chalkboard and chalk

Directions:
1. Prior to playing the game, write the titles of famous books and songs on the index cards.
2. Divide the class into two teams and have them sit on opposite sides of the room.
3. One player from each team comes to the front of the room to be a "drawer." They are shown one of the index cards "secretly."
4. The "drawers" then try to draw clues on the board to help their teammates guess what was on the index card. They may *not* write words.
5. The first team to guess their title wins a point for their team.
6. The game continues and points are tallied at the end of the playing time.

CHARADES

Skill: cooperation

Materials:
* index cards
* markers

Directions:
1. Write animals, book titles, phrases, song titles, or words on the index cards.
2. Divide the class into two teams and have them sit with their backs to each other.
3. One child from each team comes forward and is shown a card. These two stand in front of their teams and try to act out what was on their card without using words or sounds.
4. The team that guesses correctly first wins a point, and the game continues.

Adaptation:
* Older children will have fun playing this game using the names of commercial products or famous athletes.

246

CONCENTRATION

Skill: classification

Materials: none

Directions:

1. Have the children join you in this rhythm:

slap, slap	(*slap thighs*)
snap, snap	(*snap right hand, then left*)
slap, slap	(*slap thighs*)
snap, snap	(*snap right hand, then left*)
(and so on)	

2. Say each line of the following chant on the finger snaps. You should be silent as you slap your thighs.

   Concentration.
   Are you ready?
   Get set.
   Let's go.
   Colors . . .

3. As you go around the group, everyone must name a color when it is his or her turn on the "snap, snap." If someone can't think of anything to say, the game stops and you begin again with another category.

Adaptation:

    ✱ You can use categories such as mammals, plants, authors, names, or anything else.

 # TV

Skill: initial consonant sounds

Materials: ✱ chalkboard, chalk

Directions:

1. Draw the outline of a television on the chalkboard.
2. One child is "it" and comes to the front of the room. He or she writes the initials of a TV show in the television.
3. Classmates try to guess the name of the show. The first one to do so gets to be the next "it."

Adaptation:

    ✱ This game may also be played using the initials of famous people, songs, and movies.

DINOSAUR HUNT

Skill: oral language

Materials: none

Directions:
1. Have the children sit in a circle on the floor or outside on the ground.
2. Tell them to repeat each line of this chant and imitate the actions after you do them:

> Going on a dinosaur hunt. (*slap thighs*)
> And I'm not afraid. (*points to self*)
> There's a tall mountain. (*look with hand over eyes*)
> Can't go under it. (*move hand down*)
> Can't go around it. (*move hand around*)
> Guess I'll go over it. (*reach hands as if climbing*)
> There's a river. (*hands over eyes*)
> Can't go over it. (*move hand over*)
> Can't go under it. (*move hand under*)
> Guess I'll swim across it. (*move arms as if swimming*)
> There's some tall grass. (*hand over eyes*)
> Can't go over it. (*move hand over*)
> Can't go around it. (*move hand around*)
> Guess I'll go through it. (*slap hands up and down in front*)
> There's a cave. (*hand over eyes*)
> Can't go over it. (*move hand over*)
> Can't go under it. (*move hand under*)
> Guess I'll go in it.
> It's dark and spooky in here. (*shake*)
> It's cold in here. (*wrap arms around self and shiver*)
> I feel some scales. (*pretend to rub something*)
> I feel some big teeth. (*pretend to touch something*)
> Ohhh! It's a Dinosaur! (*scream!*)
> Run out of the cave. (*slap thighs*)
> Go through the grass. (*slap hands*)
> Swim across the river. (*stroke with arms*)
> Climb the mountain. (*reach with arms*)
> Run home. (*slap thighs*)
> Open the door. (*pretend to open*)
> Jump in bed. (*cover head with arms as if hiding under a blanket*)
> I went on a dinosaur hunt,
> And I wasn't afraid. (*point to self with thumbs as if boasting*)

Adaptation: ✱ This is similar to "Going on a Bear Hunt" and can be told in many different ways. You can change the words to hunt for a lion, tiger, monster, or anything you want!

 **RELAYS**

Skill:	large-motor movement; cooperation
Materials:	none
Directions:	1. Divide the class into teams with five or six players each.
	2. Have the players line up single file behind a line and run one at a time to a designated point and back. The first player tags the second player, who then runs the distance.
	3. The first team to have all players run is the winner.
Adaptations:	* Other relay games children will enjoy are:

Ball Relays: Have the children pass a ball over their heads and under their legs. The last person runs to the front of the line and continues passing over and under. When the first person is in his or her original position, their team wins the game. Relays where children must dribble a ball, kick a ball, or throw a ball into a target can also be played.

Animal Relays: Let the children walk like crabs, monkeys, bears, birds, or elephants.

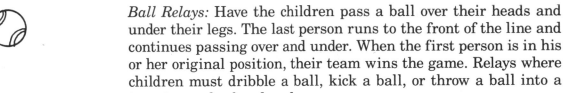

Quick Change: Prepare a bag with a shirt, pants, and hat for each team. The first player puts the clothes on, runs to a designated point, takes the clothes off, then runs and gives the clothes to the second person.

Movements: Have the children hop, jump, skip, gallop, walk backwards, and do other movements.

Pig Relay: Move a ball with your nose.

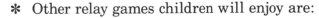

Wet T-Shirt Relay: Give children a T-shirt and have them run to a pail of water, dip the T-shirt in the water, then run and give it to the second person.

Toesie Relay: Have the children take their shoes off, pick up a peanut with their toes, carry it to a basket, and drop it in.

Potato Relay: Ask the children to carry a potato in a large spoon without dropping it.

Balloon Relay: Have the children run with a balloon to a chair, then sit on the balloon and pop it.

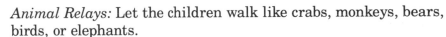

 **HUG TAG**

Skill: socialization

Materials: none

Directions:

1. Designate a playing area. One child is "it." "It" chases the other children who must "freeze" when they are tagged.
2. Players hug those who are "frozen" to "unfreeze" them.

Adaptations:

* These are a few variations of tag:

   Stoop Tag: Children stoop down on the ground when they are tagged.

   Cartoon Tag: Children must name a cartoon show when they are tagged.

   Shadow Tag: Children must freeze when "it" steps on their shadow.

   Sticky Tag: Children must hold the part of their body that is tagged.

 ANIMAL MOVEMENTS

Skill: large-motor movement

Materials:

* animal stickers or pictures of animals
* cardboard, glue, scissors

Directions:

1. Attach pictures of different animals to cardboard squares.
2. One child chooses a card, then the rest of the class must move around on the playground like that animal.

Adaptation:

* Call "land," "air," or "water" and let the children move like animals in those habitats.

ADVENTURE WALK

Skill: large-motor movement; imagination

Materials: * playground equipment

Directions: 1. Tell the children you are going to take them on an adventure walk.
                    2. First, they must climb a tall mountain. (Children climb up the slide one at a time and go down.)
                    3. Next, we must cross a river. (Jump across the sidewalk.)
                    4. Now we must go over a narrow bridge. (Walk across the balance beam.)
                    5. Here's a cave. (Climb under a piece of equipment.)
                    6. We have to go through the swamp. Don't let the alligators get you! (Crawl through a tire swing.)

Adaptations: * Make your own adventures using the equipment, trees, and other natural objects on your playground.
                    * Hide a stuffed animal or box of animal crackers to surprise the children at the end of the walk.

SNEAKY SNAKE

Skill: large-motor movement

Materials: none

Directions: 1. Have the children hold hands and stand in a long line.
                    2. Hold the child's hand at the front of the line and move them in zigzags, spirals, and all around as the others follow behind.

Adaptation: * See if the "head" of the snake can catch the "tail" of the snake.

ROCKETS

Skill: large-motor movement

Materials: none

Directions:
1. Draw two lines about 30 feet apart. Have all the children stand behind one line. A "commander" is chosen to stand behind the other line.
2. The "commander" tells the rockets to get on their launching pads, and all the children squat down. The "commander" then counts down backwards from 10 to 0 as the "rockets" gradually rise to a standing position. When the "commander" gets to 0, all the children blast off and run to the opposite line. The first one to cross the line becomes the next "commander."

HOWDY PARTNER

Skill: large-motor movement

Materials: ✳ 2 beanbags

Directions:
1. Children form a circle.
2. Two children are each given a beanbag to balance on their heads. On a given signal, they walk around the circle in opposite directions balancing their beanbags. (If they fall off, they must stop and pick them up.) When they pass each other, they must shake hands and say, "Howdy Partner!"
3. The object of the game is to see who can be the first one back to their original spot. The first one gets to be "it" and chooses the next two children to play.

EXERCISE DICE

Skill: large-motor movement

Materials:
* 2 cube boxes
* construction paper
* markers, glue

Directions:
1. Cover the boxes with construction paper.
2. On one box write numerals from 10 to 20.
3. On the other box, write different types of exercises, such as jumping jacks, bodybends, toe touches, windmills, arm circles, knee hugs, and arm stretches.
4. Roll the dice, then have the children do the exercise that lands on top the designated times on the dice.

SQUIRRELS AND NUTS

Skill: large-motor movement

Materials:
* nut

Directions:
1. Have the children stand in a circle. Show them how to make a little cup with their hands behind their backs.
2. One child is "it" and is given the nut. "It" skips around the circle, placing the nut in one child's hands. That child then begins chasing "it" around the circle. "It" tries to get back to the chaser's spot before being caught.
3. The chaser then becomes "it" and may put the nut in another child's hands.

Adaptation:
* "Drop the hankie" is a similar game where one child skips around the circle and drops a handkerchief behind a friend. That child must pick up the hankie and chase "it" back to his or her spot.

CIRCLE SOCCER

Skill: large-motor movement

Materials: * playground ball

Directions:
1. Have the children stand in a circle and hold hands.
2. Place a ball inside the circle. The children try to kick the ball and keep it inside the circle. If the ball goes out of the circle between two people, then both people are out of the game. If a player kicks the ball too high and it goes over someone's head, then the player who kicked the ball is also out of the game.
3. The game continues until there are just one or two players left.

WHAT'S THAT JIVE?
(similar to Red Rover)

Skill: large-motor movement

Materials: none

Directions:
1. Divide the children into two teams and have them stand in a line facing each other (30 to 40 feet apart).
2. One team calls for a player from the other team with this chant:
   > (*Child's name*), (*child's name*)
   > What's that jive?
   > Come on over
   > And give me five.
3. The team calling the chant holds their hands out in front of them with their palms up. The child called proceeds down their line giving each child "five" by slapping their palms. If the child who is "it" slaps the palms and then slaps under their palms, that child chases "it" back to his or her original team. If "it" is caught, he or she must return to the opposing team, but if not, the chaser must join "it's" team.
4. The game continues with teams taking turns calling players from the opposite team.

 HOT POTATO

Skill:	large-motor movement
Materials:	* ball * whistle
Directions:	1. Children stand in a circle and pass around the ball (hot potato). 2. When you blow the whistle, the child holding the ball must leave the circle. 3. The game is played until there is just one child left standing.
Adaptation:	* This game can be adapted easily to play inside. Have the children sit in a circle and pass a beanbag while you play music. When the music stops, the one holding the beanbag is out of the game.

 MOTHER, MAY I?

Skill:	large-motor movement
Materials:	none
Directions:	1. Children line up with their backs to a wall. 2. One person is "mother" and stands about 30 feet in front of the others. 3. One at a time "mother" names a child and tells them a different motion they must perform. For example: baby steps, scissor steps, twirls, giant steps, or frog leaps. The child must remember to ask "Mother, May I?" before performing the movement or he or she is sent back to the starting line. 4. The first one to reach "mother" becomes the next "mother."

 NAME BALL

Skill: large-motor movement

Materials:
* ball

Directions:
1. Have the children stand in a circle.
2. You stand in the middle of the circle with the ball, throw the ball in the air, and call out a child's name.
3. That child tries to run forward and catch the ball after one bounce.
4. The game continues as you call different children's names.

Adaptation:
* Let the children throw the ball and call their classmates' names.

© 1994 by The Center for Applied Research in Education

 CALL BALL

Skill: large-motor movement

Materials:
* ball

Directions:
1. Divide the class into two teams and have them form two lines about 30 feet apart.
2. Give each child a number by having them count off. (Two players on opposing teams will have the same number.)
3. You stand between the two teams, call out a number, and throw the ball in the air. The first child with that number to catch the ball wins a point for their team.

GROUND BASKETBALL

Skill:	large-motor movement
Materials:	* large box or laundry basket
	* ball
Directions:	1. Have the children form a circle with the basket or box placed in the middle.
	2. Have the children take turns trying to throw the ball into the basket as they pass the ball around the circle.
Adaptation:	* Divide the children into two teams and let them try to make points for their team by throwing the ball into the basket.

WOLF AND CHICKENS

Skill:	large-motor movement
Materials:	none
Directions:	1. Two lines are drawn approximately 40 feet apart.
	2. The children are the "chickens" and line up behind one of the lines. You or another child is the wolf and stands between the two lines.
	3. The wolf pretends to be a chicken and says, "cluck, cluck" and flaps arms. But when the wolf shouts, "wolf," all the chickens must run to the other line. If the wolf tags them, they must then become wolves, too, and help the wolf catch the other chickens.
	4. The game continues until all the chickens are caught. The last one caught becomes the wolf for the next game.
Adaptation:	* A similar game called "sharks and minnows" can be played. Have the minnows get behind a line as the shark tries to catch them when "shark attack" is called.

DODGE BALL

Skill: large-motor movement

Materials:
* ball

Directions:
1. Draw a large circle on the ground with a stick and have all the children stand in the circle.
2. Choose two children to stand outside the circle and roll the ball at the children in the circle.
3. The children try to "dodge" the ball as it is thrown, but they must leave the game if they are hit with the ball.
4. The game proceeds until there are two children left in the circle who become the ball throwers for the next game.

Adaptations:
* As the children are hit with the ball, they may stand outside the circle and take turns throwing the ball.
* A similar game called "sticky ball" can be played. Children must stick their hand to the part of their body hit by the ball. After being hit three times, they are out of the game.

CAT AND MOUSE

Skill: cooperation

Materials: none

Directions:
1. The children form a circle and hold hands. One child stands in the center and is the "mouse." Another child stands outside the circle and is the "cat."
2. On a given signal, the "cat" must chase the "mouse." They may enter or leave the circle only if the other players hold up their arms to form an arch.
3. When the "cat" catches the "mouse," let them choose a classmate to take their place.

Adaptation:
* Change the characters in the game for different holidays or seasons. You could have the farmer chase the turkey, the snowman chase his hat, and so forth.

 **RED LIGHT**

Skill: large-motor movement

Materials: none

Directions:
1. Two lines are drawn 30 feet apart. The children stand behind one line, while "it" stands on the opposite line.
2. "It" turns his or her back to the other players and calls out, "One, two, three, red light!" The players run toward "it," but must stop on the word "red light." On this signal, "it" turns and faces the other players. If anyone is caught moving, the player is sent back to the starting line.
3. The first one to tag "it" becomes the new leader.

 **STATUE**

Skill: large-motor movement

Materials: none

Directions:
1. Divide the children into groups of four or five.
2. Each group thinks of a statue they can make with their bodies. (Let them think of a title for their statue, too.)
3. Groups perform their statue for their classmates, while classmates try to guess what their title is.

Adaptation:
* Increase the size of the groups to see how many people they can incorporate into their statue.

FOLLOW THE LEADER

Skill: large-motor movement

Materials: none

Directions:

1. One person is chosen to be the leader. The rest of the class must get behind the leader and do just what the leader does.
2. The leader walks, hops, runs, skips, waves his or her hands in the air, goes under something, slides down the slide, and so forth.
3. After several minutes another child is chosen to be leader.

 # JUMP THE CREEK

Skill: large-motor movement

Materials: * 2 jump ropes

Directions:

1. Place the two ropes on the ground a few inches apart to make a creek.
2. Have the children line up single file and try to jump over the creek one at a time without stepping on a rope.
3. After every child has jumped, move the ropes a little farther apart to make the creek wider.
4. Continue moving the ropes farther apart and letting the children jump over them. When a player can no longer jump over the ropes, they must stand to the side of the game and be cheerleaders.
5. The object of the game is to see how far the children can jump.

Adaptation: * You can play a similar game by drawing lines in the sand or dirt.

FOLLOW ME

Skill: large-motor movement

Materials: none

Directions:

1. Children form a circle, face right, and extend their right arm out.
2. One player is "it" and runs around the outside of the circle. "It" touches someone's arm and says "follow me" and that child begins to run around the circle, too.
3. The second player touches another player's arm, says "follow me," and the game continues until 5 to 10 children are running around the outside of the circle. "It" yells "home" and all the players try to get to their space. The player left without a space becomes the next "it."

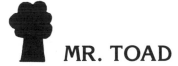

MR. TOAD

Skill: large-motor movement

Materials: none

Directions:

1. One child is "Mr. Toad" and stands away from the group.
2. The rest of the class stands on a line about 30 feet from Mr. Toad.
3. The children ask in unison, "Mr. Toad, what time is it?" Mr. Toad offers a time between one and twelve o'clock. The children get to jump that number of times. For example, if Mr. Toad says "5 o'clock," they jump 5 times.
4. Continue the game until one child reaches Mr. Toad. That child then gets to be the toad.

SILENT BALL

Skill: large-motor movement

Materials: * ball

Directions:
1. Have the children form a circle.
2. Give one child the ball. He or she throws it to another child without calling the child's name or saying anything.
3. If a child fails to catch the ball or drops the ball, the child is out of the game.
4. Continue throwing the ball silently until there are just two players left.

BOUNDARY BALL

Skill: large-motor movement

Materials: * 2 balls

Directions:

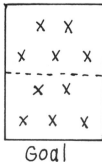

1. Divide the class into two teams.
2. Draw two lines about 40 feet apart. Draw a center line between them.
3. Each team spreads out in half of the playing area and faces the middle center line.
4. Give each team a ball to try to bounce or roll over the other team's back line. Players try to move around to keep the ball from going over their line.
5. The first team to get their ball over their opponent's line wins a point.

© 1994 by The Center for Applied Research in Education

DOG CATCHER

© 1994 by The Center for Applied Research in Education

Skill: large-motor movement

Materials: none

Directions:

1. Draw two lines about 30 feet apart.
2. Name three or four different kinds of dogs, such as a cocker spaniel, scottie, beagle, or poodle. Each child decides what kind of dog he or she wants to be. The dogs stand in their "kennel" behind one of the lines.
3. One child is selected to be the "dog catcher." The dog catcher calls out one kind of dog, and those dogs run to the opposite line. If they are caught, they are put in the pound.
4. The last child caught becomes the new dog catcher.

BACK TO BACK

Skill: large-motor movement; cooperation

Materials: none

Directions:

1. One child is "it," and the other players move around in a designated area.
2. When "it" yells "back to back," all the players must find a partner and touch backs with them. When "it" says "face to face," the partners turn around and shake hands.
3. Players begin moving around again. When "back to back" is called, they must find a new partner. "It" tries to get a partner, too, and the child left out becomes the new "it."

STEAL THE BACON

Skill: large-motor movement

Materials: * eraser, stick, or other small object

Directions:

1. Divide the class into two teams and have them stand behind two lines about 40 feet apart.
2. Have the children number off on each team.
3. Place the "bacon" (eraser or stick) between the two teams, then call out a number. The two children with that number try to "steal the bacon" and run with it back to their line without being tagged by the other player. The child who successfully does this gets a point for their team, but if they are tagged in the process, the other player earns a point for his or her team.
4. The team with more points after all the numbers are called wins the game.

 COLOR SQUARES

Skill: large-motor movement

Materials: * 8 sheets of construction paper in different colors

Directions:

1. Place the sheets of construction paper around in a circle.
2. One child is "it" and stands in the middle of the circle. The other players march around the colors.
3. "It" calls out a color and all the players scramble to line up behind it. The last player to get there becomes the next "it."

DUCK–DUCK–GOOSE

Skill: large-motor movement

Materials: none

Directions:
1. Children form a circle and one child is chosen to be "it."
2. "It" walks around the outside of the circle saying "duck" as he or she touches each player. Players squat down as they are tapped.
3. If "it" touches a child and says "goose," that child must chase "it" around the circle before "it" can get back to "goose's" place. If "it" is caught, he or she must sit in the center of the circle. "Goose" then becomes "it" and the game continues.

BUILD THE CASTLE

Skill: large-motor movement

Materials: * long jump rope

Directions:
1. Choose two people to hold the rope.
2. The other players form a straight line and take turns jumping over the rope. The rope begins on the ground, but after everyone has had a turn it is raised a few inches. If a child's foot touches the rope, he or she is out of the game.
3. Continue raising the rope until there is just one child left who can jump the height.

Adaptation: * A similar game called "school" can be played. When the rope is on the ground it is called "kindergarten." Each time the rope is raised it is called "first grade," "second grade," and so on.

 MIDNIGHT

Skill: large-motor movement

Materials: none

Directions:
1. Draw two lines about 40 feet apart. The children pretend to be sheep and stand in their "fold" behind one line.
2. One child is chosen to be the "fox." The "fox" stands in its "den" behind the opposite line.
3. The "fox" and the "sheep" come out and start wandering around in the "meadow" between the two lines. The sheep asks the fox, "What time is it?", and the fox answers, "Five o'clock," or "nine o'clock," and so forth. When the fox answers, "Midnight," all the sheep scramble for their fold.
4. The sheep tagged become foxes and the game continues until there is one sheep left, who then becomes the new fox.

 LIMBO

Skill: large-motor movement

Materials: * broomstick or similar long stick

Directions:
1. Select two children to hold the broomstick at chest level.
2. Let the rest of the children form a line and take turns wiggling under the broomstick. If they touch it, they are out of the game.
3. Continue lowering the broomstick until there is just one child left, then begin the game again.

Adaptation: * Play some lively music for the children to dance to as they do the limbo.

JUMP ROPE RHYMES

Jumping rope is a terrific form of exercise that will be even more fun with these rhymes.

Bubble Gum

Bubble gum, bubble gum in a dish.
How many pieces do you wish?
One, two, three, four . . .
(*Continue counting until the child misses.*)

Teddy Bear

Teddy bear, teddy bear, turn around.
Teddy bear, teddy bear, touch the ground.
Teddy bear, teddy bear, tie your shoes.
Teddy bear, teddy bear, read the news.
Teddy bear, teddy bear, climb the stairs.
Teddy bear, teddy bear, say your prayers.
Teddy bear, teddy bear, turn off the lights.
Teddy bear, teddy bear, say good night.
(*Child acts out various motions while jumping.*)

Blue Bells

Blue bells, cockle shells,
Eevy, ivy, over.
(*Swing rope back and forth as you say this
chant when the child begins to jump.*)

Down in the Valley

Down in the valley where the green grass grows.
There sat (*child's name*) as sweet as a rose.
She sang and she sang and she sang so sweet.
Along came (*sweetheart's name*) and
Kissed her on the cheek.
How many kisses did she receive?
One, two, three, four . . .
(*Continue counting until the child misses.*)

Engine Number Nine

Engine, engine, number nine
Coming down the railroad line.
If the train jumps off the track,
You will get your money back.
How much money will you receive?
One, two, three, four . . .
(*Continue counting until the child misses.*)

Cinderella

Cinderella, dressed in yella,
Went upstairs to meet her fella.
Made a mistake and kissed a snake.
How many doctors did it take?
One, two, three, four . . .
(*Continue counting until the child misses.*)

Down by the Ocean

Down by the ocean,
Down by the sea,
(*Child's name*) broke a bottle
And blamed it on me.
I told ma—ma told pa.
How many lectures
Did I receive?
One, two, three, four . . .
(*Continue counting until the child misses.*)

Super Snacks and Silly Songs

Most children will agree that it tastes better when you fix it yourself. These recipes can be used with a small group, as a self-serve snack in a learning center, or enlarged for a language experience chart. There's even a silly song to go along with each recipe.

MONKEY SANDWICH

Skill: good nutrition; independence

Materials:
* hotdog buns
* peanut butter
* banana
* plastic utensils, napkins

Directions:
1. Wash your hands.
2. Spread peanut butter in the hotdog bun.
3. Peel the banana and place it in the hotdog bun.
4. Cut the monkey sandwich in half and share it with a good friend.
5. Enjoy!
6. Clean up.

Adaptations:
* Act out the fingerplay below about five little monkeys:

Five little monkeys	(*Hold up 5 fingers.*)
Hanging in a tree,	
Teasing Mr. Alligator,	(*Point finger.*)
"You can't catch me.	
"You can't catch me."	
Along comes Mr. Alligator	(*Put hands together to
Quiet as can be and	make alligator mouth.*)
Snap!	(*Clap hands.*)

Four little monkeys . . .
Three little monkeys . . .
Two little monkeys . . .
One little monkey . . .
(*After Mr. Alligator snaps
that last little monkey he
says, "I'm full!"*)

* Serve tuna salad, chicken salad, cheese, and other sandwich fillings in hotdog buns.

© 1994 by The Center for Applied Research in Education

MUNCH MIX

Skill: good nutrition; counting

Materials:
* raisins
* pretzel sticks
* fish crackers
* Cheerios™
* peanuts or M&M's™ (optional)
* ice cream cones
* sandwich bag
* napkins

Directions:
1. Wash your hands.
2. Count out 10 of each item and put them in your bag.
3. Shake it up, then pour it in your ice cream cone.
4. Munch and enjoy. When you're through with the mix, you can eat the cone.

Adaptations:
* You can also prepare this in a large bowl and spoon it into the cones.
* This is a great snack on nature hikes or field trips because there's no mess or trash.
* You can add miniature marshmallows, sunflower seeds, dried fruit, carob chips, or anything else you want to add to this mix.
* Sing this song as you count:

> One little, two little, three little raisins . . .
> Four little, five little, six little raisins . . .
> Seven little, eight little, nine little raisins . . .
> Ten little raisins to munch.
>
> One little, two little, three little pretzels . . .
> Cheerios™ . . .
> Peanuts . . .

FROZEN JUICE POPS

Skill: good nutrition

Materials:
* fruit juice
* paper cups
* popsicle sticks
* napkins

Directions:
1. Wash your hands.
2. Fill the cups ⅔ full with fruit juice.
3. Put a popsicle stick in the cups, put the cups in a pan, then place them in the freezer.
4. After the pops have frozen, remove the paper and enjoy.

Adaptations:
* You can use orange juice, grape juice, apple juice, or most any type of juice for this activity.
* Make tiny pops by freezing the juice in ice cube trays and using a toothpick instead of a popsicle stick.
* Mix plain yogurt with frozen juice concentrate and freeze to make a yummy and healthy snack.
* Cool off with this song that can be sung to the tune of "Sailing, Sailing, Over the Bounding Maine":

Swimming, swimming	*(Stroke arms as swimming.)*
In the swimming pool.	*(Make pool with palms of hands.)*
When days are hot	*(Fan self.)*
Or days are cool	*(Shiver.)*
In the swimming pool.	*(Make pool with hands.)*
Back stroke,	*(Swim backwards.)*
Side stroke,	*(Do the side stroke.)*
Fancy diving, too.	*(Pretend to dive.)*
There's no place	*(Shake head no.)*
I would rather be	*(Point to self.)*
Than in the	*(Make pool with hands.)*
Swimming pool.	

(Each time you sing the song leave out another line and just hum the tune as you do the motions.)

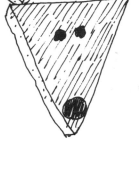

REINDEER SANDWICH

Skill: good nutrition; following directions

Materials:
* bread
* peanut butter
* pretzel twists
* raisins
* red candies
* napkins

Directions:
1. Wash your hands.
2. Cut the bread into a triangle.
3. Spread peanut butter on the triangle.
4. Use raisins for the eyes and a piece of red candy for the nose.
5. Break the pretzels in half and add for antlers.
6. Eat and enjoy!
7. Clean up.

Adaptations:

* You can sing "Rudolph the Red Nosed Reindeer" before you eat your sandwich. Make a reindeer puppet from a lunch bag. Trace around your hands on black construction paper and use these for the antlers.
* Here's a new song to the tune of "We Wish You a Merry Christmas":

> Let's all do a little clapping.
> Let's all do a little clapping.
> Let's all do a little clapping,
> To spread holiday cheer.
>
> Let's all do a little jumping . . .
> Let's all do a little twirling . . .
> Let's all do a little hugging . . .
> Let's all do a little snapping . . .
> (*Make up your own fun verses.*)

 FRIED WORMS

Skill: small-motor movement

Materials:
* Tootsie™ rolls
* graham crackers
* plastic sandwich bags
* napkins

Directions:
1. Wash your hands.
2. Put a graham cracker in the plastic bag and crumble it.
3. Roll the Tootsie™ roll between your hands until it looks like a worm.
4. Shake the "worm" in the graham cracker crumbs.
5. Eat your fried "worm."
6. Clean up.

Adaptation:
* Here's a song to sing as you eat your worm:

> Nobody loves me.
> Everybody hates me.
> Guess I'll go eat worms.
> Short, fat, squishy ones,
> Long, skinny, slimy ones.
> See how they wiggle
> And squirm.

WALKING SALAD

Skill: good nutrition

Materials:
* small apples
* peanut butter
* raisins
* napkins, spoons

Directions:
1. Wash your hands.
2. Wash and core the apple. (CAUTION: Coring should be done by an adult.)
3. Spoon peanut butter into the center of the apple.
4. Sprinkle raisins on top.
5. Yummy!
6. Clean up.

Adaptations:

* Take two slices of a red apple. Spread peanut butter on one slice, then place 3 or 4 miniature marshmallows on top of the peanut butter. Put the other apple slice on top of the marshmallows and you'll have a smile sandwich.
* Did you know that there's a little star inside every apple? Slice an apple diagonally, open it up, and you'll find a star.
* Here's a finger play to go along with apple snacks:

Way up high	(*Point up in the air.*)
In the apple tree,	
Two red apples	(*Hold up 2 fingers.*)
Smiled down at me.	(*Look down.*)
I shook that tree	(*Pretend to shake tree.*)
As hard as I could,	
And down came the apples.	(*Move arms in downward motion.*)
Mmmm! Mmmm! Good!	(*Pat tummy.*)

SILLY FACE SANDWICH

Skill: good nutrition; independence

Materials:
- * bread
- * circle cookie cutter
- * shredded carrots
- * raisins
- * cherry
- * peanut butter
- * napkins, plastic knife

Directions:
1. Wash your hands.
2. Cut a circle from a slice of bread.
3. Spread peanut butter on the circle.
4. Add shredded carrots for hair, raisins for eyes, and a cherry for a mouth.
5. Think of a name for your silly sandwich.
6. Gobble it up!
7. Clean up.

Adaptations:
- * Use dried fruits or miniature marshmallows for facial features.
- * Sing this song about body parts to the tune of "The Wheels on the Bus":

You take your little eyes	(*Point to eyes.*)
And go blink, blink, blink.	(*Blink eyes.*)
Blink, blink, blink.	
Blink, blink, blink.	
You take your little eyes	
And go blink, blink, blink.	
Blink, blink, blink.	
Lips—kiss.	(*Make smacking sound with your lips.*)
Nose—sniff.	(*Pretend to sniff with nose.*)
Hands—clap.	(*Clap hands and for the last line sing "and put them in your lap."*)

FRUIT KABOBS

Skill: good nutrition

Materials:
* grapes, strawberries, banana slices, pineapple chunks (almost any fruit will work)
* toothpicks or wooden skewers
* napkins, plastic knife

Directions:
1. Wash your hands.
2. Clean the fruit and cut into bite-size pieces.
3. Skewer the fruit on the toothpicks.
4. Enjoy!
5. Clean up.

Adaptations:
* Have the children count sets of each type of fruit.
* Ask the children to reproduce a pattern on their kabobs.
* Wash and freeze grapes for a cool treat on a hot day.
* Frozen bananas are another refreshing treat. Peel the banana. Cut it in half. Insert a popsicle stick in each half, then place on a cookie sheet and put in the freezer.
* Try singing this silly song to the tune of "When the Saints Go Marching In":

> I like to eat. I like to eat.
> I like to eat apples and bananas.
> Oh, I like to eat.
> I like to eat apples and bananas.
>
> (*Sing the second verse, inserting the long A sound for every vowel, like this.*)
>
> A lake ta ate. A lake ta ate.
> A lake ta ate applas and bananas.
> A, A lake ta ate.
> A lake ta ate applas and bananas.
>
> (*Sing with the long e, i, o, and u sounds.*)

TORTILLA ROLL-UP

Skill: good nutrition; following directions

Materials:
* small flour tortillas
* sliced sandwich meat (thin)
* sliced cheese
* mayonnaise or mustard
* napkins, plastic utensils

Directions:
1. Wash your hands.
2. Spread mayonnaise or mustard on the tortilla.
3. Place a piece of meat and cheese on the tortilla.
4. Roll up the tortilla.
5. Slice diagonally into bite-size pieces. (Secure with a toothpick if you desire.)
6. Mmmmmmm! Muy bueno!
7. Clean up.

Adaptations:
* Use cream cheese or other fillings on tortillas.
* Here's a song to sing to the tune of "Shortnin' Bread" as you make your sandwich:

> Everybody do this, do this, do this.
> Everybody do this just like me.
>
> Put on the mayonnaise, mayonnaise, mayonnaise.
> Put on the mayonnaise just like me.
>
> Add some meat, meat, meat.
> Add some meat just like me.
>
> Next there's cheese, cheese, cheese.
> Next there's cheese, add it, please.
>
> Roll up your sandwich, sandwich, sandwich.
> Roll up your sandwich just like me.
>
> Eat your sandwich, sandwich, sandwich.
> Mmmmmmmmmmmmmm (*hum this last line*).
>
> (*You can make up lots of different verses to this song to get children to hop, clap, jump, or do other motions.*)

ANTS ON A LOG

Skill: good nutrition

Materials:
* celery
* cream cheese
* raisins
* napkins, plastic utensils

Directions:
1. Wash your hands.
2. Clean the celery and cut into 3" pieces.
3. Spread cream cheese into the hollow part of the celery.
4. Put "ants" (raisins) on the "log" (celery).
5. Crunch and munch.
6. Clean up.

Adaptations:
* Spread peanut butter on the celery in place of the cream cheese and top with the raisins.
* Fill the celery with pimento cheese.
* Here's an old favorite about ants:

The ants go marching one by one,	(*Hold up 1 finger.*)
Hur-rah, hur-rah.	(*Cheer.*)
The ants go marching one by one,	(*Hold up 1 finger.*)
Hur-rah, hur-rah.	(*Cheer.*)
The ants go marching one by one,	(*Hold up 1 finger.*)
The little one stops to suck his thumb.	(*Suck thumb.*)
And they all go marching	(*March feet.*)
Down to the ground	(*Point down.*)
To get out of the rain,	(*Point down.*)
Boom! Boom! Boom!	(*Clap hands.*)

Two . . . tie his shoe
Three . . . climb a tree
Four . . . shut the door
Five . . . take a dive
Six . . . pick up sticks
Seven . . . pray to heaven
Eight . . . shut the gate
Nine . . . check the time
Ten . . . they all say let's do it again!

PUMPKIN SANDWICH

Skill: good nutrition; independence

Materials:
* bread
* circle cookie cutter
* softened cream cheese
* food coloring
* raisins
* napkins, plastic utensils

Directions:

1. Wash your hands.
2. Cut out a circle from a slice of bread.
3. Mix the cream cheese with a few drops red and yellow food coloring to make it orange.
4. Spread the cream cheese on the bread.
5. Use the raisins to make a pumpkin face.
6. Eat and enjoy!
7. Clean up.

Adaptations:

* Sing this song to the tune of "Lassie and Laddie" as you make your sandwich:

> Oh, once I had a pumpkin, a pumpkin, a pumpkin.
> Oh, once I had a pumpkin with no face at all.
> With no eyes, and no nose,
> And no mouth, and no teeth.
> Oh, once I had a pumpkin with no face at all.
>
> So I made a jack-o'-lantern, jack-o'-lantern,
> Jack-o'-lantern.
> So I made a jack-o'-lantern with a big, funny face
> With big eyes and a big nose,
> And a big mouth and big teeth.
> So I made a jack-o'-lantern with a big, funny face.

* Use other holiday cookie colors and tint the cream cheese or other filling accordingly. Decorate with raisins, miniature marshmallows, peanuts, candies, sunflower seeds, or dried fruits.

(pink)   (green)   (blue)

DIRT CAKE

Skill: following directions

Materials:
* instant chocolate pudding
* Cool-Whip™
* Oreos™
* gummy worms
* clear plastic cups
* napkins, plastic spoons

Directions:
1. Wash your hands.
2. Prepare the pudding according to the directions on the package.
3. Crush the Oreos™.
4. Layer pudding, Cool-Whip™, and crushed cookies in the cup.
5. Add a gummy worm.
6. Mmmmm!
7. Clean up.

Adaptations:

* Sprinkle sunflower seeds and add a plastic flower just for fun.
* Make a similar treat called "sand cakes" with instant vanilla pudding, Cool-Whip™, vanilla wafers, and gummy fish or sharks.
* Sing this song to the tune of "Pop Goes the Weasel":

You put a seed *(Make fist with left hand*
Down in the ground, *and insert right index finger.)*
And then you have *(Wiggle fingers down in front*
A shower. *of you like rain.)*
The sun shines *(Make a sun over your head*
Bright all around. *with your arms.)*
Up comes a flower! *(Bring right arm up through*
left fist.)

SPIDER SANDWICH

Skill: good nutrition; independence

Materials:
* whole wheat bread
* circle cookie cutter
* peanut butter or other favorite filling
* pretzel sticks
* raisins
* napkins, plastic utensils

Directions:
1. Wash your hands.
2. Cut 2 circles from the bread.
3. Spread peanut butter or other favorite filling on one circle, then top with the other circle.
4. Insert 4 pretzels on either side for legs.
5. Add raisins for eyes or mouth.
6. Eat and enjoy!
7. Clean up.

Adaptations:
* Sing the "Eensy Weensy Spider" with a regular verse. Sing the "Big, Fat Spider" with a loud voice and big motions. Sing the "Eeensy Weensy Spider" with a tiny voice and smaller motions.
* Use cheese sticks or carrot sticks for legs.

© 1994 by The Center for Applied Research in Education

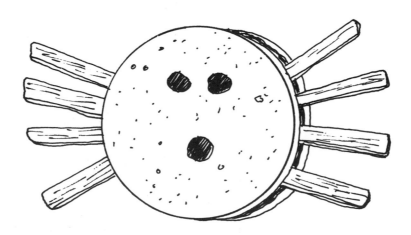

TIN CAN ICE CREAM

Skill: cooperation

Materials:
* homemade ice cream mixture
* crushed ice
* ice cream salt
* masking tape
* 1-lb. coffee can
* 2-lb. coffee can
* napkins

Directions:
1. Wash your hands.
2. Prepare your favorite homemade ice cream mixture. Pour it into the 1-lb. can and tape the top securely in place.
3. Put the smaller can in the larger can, then pack it with layers of ice and salt. Place the top on and tape it in place.
4. Kick the can around on the playground for about 15 minutes until the ice cream freezes.
5. Everyone will "scream" for this ice cream.

Adaptations:

* You can also use self-lock storage bags in a similar manner to freeze ice cream.
* Sing this song to "If You're Happy and You Know It":

> I wish I were a little ice cream cone.
> Oh, I wish I were a little ice cream cone.
> I'd go drippy, drippy, drippy,
> And make you sticky, sticky.
> Oh, I wish I were a little ice cream cone.
>
> I wish I were a little bit of mud . . .
> I'd go oozie, oozie, oozie,
> Between your little toosies.
>
> I wish I were a little piece of orange . . .
> I'd go squirty, squirty, squirty,
> All over your shirty.
>
> I wish I were a little piece of cake . . .
> I'd go yummy, yummy, yummy,
> In everybody's tummy.
>
> I wish I were a little radio . . .
> I'd go click. (*Turn off the song.*)

ANIMALS' PICNIC

Skill: good nutrition

Materials:
* apples
* carrots
* celery
* berries (in season)
* peanuts in shells (for older children)
* popcorn or sunflower seeds
* napkins, plastic knife

Directions:
1. Talk about foods that different animals eat. What are some foods that people eat, too?
2. Wash your hands.
3. Prepare the foods by washing the fruits and vegetables and cutting them into small pieces.
4. Go outside and have a picnic snack just like the animals do.

Adaptations:
* Have an indoor picnic if the weather is cold or rainy. Just spread a blanket on the floor and enjoy the healthy food.
* Here are some new verses to an old song, or you can make up your own words:

> I'm bringing home a baby bumblebee.
> Won't my mommy be so proud of me?
> I'm bringing home a baby bumblebee.
> Buzz–buzz–buzz–buzz–buzz.
>
> I'm bringing home a baby rattlesnake.
> Won't my mommy shiver and shake?
> I'm bringing home a baby rattlesnake.
> Ssss–Ssss–Ssss–Ssss–Ssss!
>
> I'm bringing home a little baby skunk.
> Won't my mommy hide in the trunk?
> I'm bringing home a little baby skunk.
> Stink–alink–alink–alink–alink.
>
> I'm bringing home a baby grizzly bear.
> Won't my mommy pull out all her hair?
> I'm bringing home a baby grizzly bear.
> Grrr–Grrr–Grrr–Grrr–Grrr!

ASTRONAUT PUDDING

Skill: independence

Materials:
* self-lock sandwich bag
* instant pudding
* milk
* napkins

Directions:
1. Wash your hands.
2. Put 2 tablespoons of pudding mix and ½ cup of milk in each plastic bag and zip it up.
3. Mix and squish the bag.
4. When pudding is made, poke a hole in the corner of the bag and squeeze the pudding in your mouth just like the astronauts.
5. Mmmmmm!

Adaptations:

* How about a mud pie? Put the pudding mix and milk in a plastic container with a secure top. Let the children take turns passing around the container and shaking it. Serve the pudding in a flat bottom ice cream cone and you've got a mud pie.

* Squat down on the floor and count backwards: 10–9–8–7–6–5–4–3–2–1–BLAST OFF! (*Jump up in the air as you say this.*)

* Sing this song to the tune of "Do You Know the Muffin Man?"

Do you know the astronaut,
The astronaut, the astronaut?
Do you know the astronaut
Who walks around slowly like this?

(Pretend to be an astronaut and move slowly.)

Yes, we know the astronaut,
The astronaut, the astronaut.
Yes, we know the astronaut
Who walks around slowly like this.

(Let children take turns demonstrating how different animals and people move as you sing this song.)

FIRE CRACKER SANDWICH

Skill: good nutrition; following directions

Materials:
* bread
* peanut butter, cream cheese, tuna salad
* rolling pin
* plastic wrap
* curling ribbon or yarn
* napkins, plastic utensils

Directions:
1. Wash your hands.
2. Cut the crusts from a piece of bread.
3. Roll the bread flat with the rolling pin.
4. Spread your favorite filling on the bread.
5. Tightly roll up the sandwich.
6. Wrap in plastic and tie the ends with ribbon to resemble a fire cracker.
7. It'll be a *blast* when you eat it!
8. Clean up.

Adaptation:
* Do this "Yankee Doodle" dance before you eat your sandwich:

Yankee Doodle Went to town Riding on A pony. He stuck a Feather in His cap And called it Macaroni.	*(Put one foot out in* *front of the other* *and rock back and forth* *to the beat of the music.* *Hold hands in front of* *you as if holding the* *reins of a horse.)* *(Put feet together and* *put hands on hips.)*
Yankee Doodle Keep it up. Yankee Doodle Dandy. Mind the music And your step And with The girls Be handy.	*(Again, rock back and* *forth as if riding a* *horse.)* *(Hop on right foot and stick* *out left heel.)* *(Hop on left foot and stick* *out right heel.)*

SECTION 10

Special Days

Are you ready for a luau, wild west round-up, olympics, or beach party? Every day will be a special day with lots of ideas from A to Z.

EVERY DAY'S A SPECIAL DAY!

Give children something to look forward to and a special memory by turning an ordinary day into one of these surprise days. Get dressed up, cook a treat, do a unique art project, bring in a guest speaker, tie in some music, play games, and think of other creative ways to make special days happy, learning times. From A to Z, here are ideas for every week of the year.

Aeronautics Day: Make paper airplanes and see how far they can fly. Invite a pilot or flight attendant to speak to the class.

Alphabet Party: Assign each child a different letter of the alphabet and ask them to bring in something from home that begins with that sound. Make letter-shaped cookies or bread.

Arbor Day: Plant a tree. Name your tree and watch it change in the different seasons.

Art Fair: Set up art stations (painting, clay, collage, puppets, jewelry) around your room or playground.

Backwards Day: Wear clothes backwards and follow your daily schedule backwards. (Don't forget to eat your dessert first at lunch!)

Banana Day: Measure with bananas, play golf with a banana, sing banana songs, and make banana splits.

Beach Party: (See activity.)

Book Party: Bring in your favorite book or dress up like your favorite character.

Bubble Day: Blow giant bubbles or do body bubble painting.

Camping Day: (See activity.)

Carnival: Divide children into small groups and let them come up with a game or activity for the carnival. (Older children may want to set up a carnival for the younger ones.)

288

**Clown or
Circus Day:**   (See activity.)

Cook-In: Let the children go to different stations and prepare foods and drinks. (You might want to have a different activity for each of the four food groups.)

Dance Contest: Let the children bring their favorite records from home and dance the day away.

**Doughnuts
with Dad:**   Invite dads in for doughnuts before they go to work. (Let children make invitations and help prepare the food. Involve dads in an art project with the children, such as finger painting or play dough.)

Earth Day: Recycle, plant trees, pick up trash, do junk art, and talk about things that we can do to care for our Earth.

Family Work Day: Plan a Saturday when parents can come in with their children and paint, clean, work on the grounds, build a play fort, or do other projects together.

Fashion Show: Plan a fashion show and invite parents.

Favorite Toy Day: Everyone brings a favorite toy from home and shares with their friends.

Friend Day: Children invite a special friend to school to visit.

Grandparents Day: Grandparents or "adopted" grandparents can come for cookies, songs, and fun.

Grown-Up Day: Children dress up like what they want to be when they grow up.

Hat Day: (See activity.)

Hollywood Day: Dress up like your favorite movie star or entertainer and play "guess who I am?"

**I-Can-Do-Something-
Special Day:**   Every child sings a song, tells a joke, shares a hobby, or tells what's special about them. (Video and send home for parents to see.)

International Day: Children wear native dress from different countries and sample ethnic foods.

EVERY DAY'S A SPECIAL DAY!, continued

Jelly Bean Day: Estimate how many jelly beans are in a jar, do jelly bean art, and play other jelly bean games.

Johnny Appleseed Day: Make homemade applesauce, taste different kinds of apples, make apple prints, and tell stories about Johnny Appleseed.

Kite Day: (See activity.)

Luau: (See activity.)

Lucky Day (Friday the 13th): Play Bingo, wear four-leaf clovers, hunt for pennies, make rabbit's feet from cardboard and cotton, and so forth.

Mardi Gras: Decorate riding toys, choose a king and queen, and have a parade where you pass out treats.

Maze Day: Set up a maze with appliance boxes and blankets.

Muffins with Mom: Make muffins and invite moms in for a little party before work.

Nature Day: Take a nature walk and do nature arts and crafts.

Office Day: Let the children dress up in clothes like their parents wear to work. You might change your classroom into an office with typewriters, telephones, paper, pens, envelopes, and computers.

Pajama Party: Children wear pajamas, bring sleeping bags, and watch videos as they eat popcorn.

Pet Day: Bring real pets (with adult supervision), stuffed animals, or pictures of pets.

Pizza Party: Make homemade pizzas.

Pumpkin Day: Everyone brings a pumpkin to decorate. Count seeds, make pumpkin bread, and brainstorm all the things you can do with a pumpkin.

Puppet Day: Make puppets, then put on a puppet show.

Queens and Kings: Make crowns for each child to decorate and let them tell you what they would do if they were a queen or king.

© 1994 by The Center for Applied Research in Education

290

Restaurant Day: Set the classroom up like a restaurant with menus, waiters and waitresses, food, and a cashier.

Robots and Inventions: Let the children design and make robots or inventions.

Skit Day: Divide the children into groups and have them put on skits for each other. They may want to dramatize a favorite story, song, or nursery rhyme.

Sock Hop: Wear funny socks and have a dance.

Sports Day: Wear shirts and hats of favorite teams and bring balls, racquets, bats, and other sports equipment to play with.

Tasting Party: Everyone brings a favorite food to share with classmates. (Encourage children to bring healthy foods and ask parents to prepare it in bite-size pieces.)

Unbirthday Party: How about a birthday party when it's everyone's "unbirthday"? Play party games, sing, and decorate cupcakes.

Volleyball Day: Play volleyball and other ball games.

Wash Day: Wear old clothes and bring sponges, pails, and squirt bottles. Let the children wash riding toys, classroom equipment, and so on.

Wild West: (See activity.)

Winter Picnic: When it's cold outside, spread a blanket on the floor and have an indoor picnic.

X Marks the Spot: Hide clues and set up a treasure hunt around the playground with a prize for everyone at the end.

Yellow Day: Children wear yellow, paint with yellow, have a yellow snack, find things that are yellow on the playground. (Change for other colors.)

Zoo Day: Go on a field trip to the zoo, or let children make homemade animal costumes and act like different animals. Serve raw apples, carrots, peanuts, and other "animal" food.

 **BEACH PARTY**

Skill: socialization

Sun Visor

Materials:
* paper plates
* scissors
* markers or crayons
* rubber bands or yarn
* stapler

Directions:

1. Cut a moon shape from the paper plate as shown.
2. Decorate with markers or crayons.
3. Attach a rubber band to each end or tie in place with yarn.

 Sun Glasses

Materials:
* plastic ring from drink cans
* colored cellophane or acetate (clear report folders work well)
* pipe cleaners
* stapler

Directions:
1. Cut off two rings.
2. Cut the cellophane or acetate the size of the outside of the rings, then staple in place.
3. Twist pipe cleaners to the outside of the ring, then bend to fit around the ears.

Adaptations:
* Wear bathing suits and have water play.
* Serve watermelon or fruit ice pops for snack.
* Play ball games with beach balls.
* Try having a beach party in the middle of winter. Ask children to wear their swimsuits, bring beach towels, and have a picnic!

 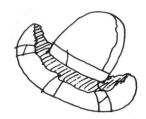

HAT DAY

Skill: socialization

Materials:
- * newspaper
- * masking tape

Directions:

1. Take 3 sheets of newspaper and put them on the child's head. Have the child hold them down.
2. Starting where the eyebrows are, wrap masking tape tightly around the head.
3. Begin rolling up the edges of the newspaper to make a brim, then tape in place.
4. Be creative! You can make bowlers, cowboy hats, fancy hats, or anything you want.

Adaptations:

- * Decorate your hats with tissue paper flowers, feathers, ribbon and lace scraps.
- * This is a wonderful activity for a carnival or family fun night to encourage parent/child interaction.
- * For hat day, you can also let children wear their favorite hats from home. Parade around the room or school with your hats on.
- * Toss beanbags into a hat or play a relay game with hats.
- * Do the Mexican Hat dance.

 **KITE DAY**

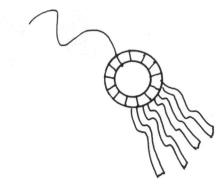

Skill: large-motor movement

Materials:
* paper plates
* markers or crayons
* tissue paper
* scissors, glue, yarn

Directions:
1. Cut out the center of the plate, leaving just the rim.
2. Decorate the rim.
3. Glue strips of tissue paper to one side of the plate.
4. Tie a piece of yarn to the other side.
5. Let's go fly a kite!

Adaptations:
* Another simple kite can be made from a paper lunch bag. Decorate the bag with crayons or markers. Punch holes in the top of the bag and tie on a 4-foot piece of yarn. Glue tissue streamers to the other end.
* Recycle a bread wrapper to make a kite.
* Make kite-shaped sandwiches.

  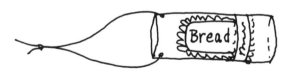

PIÑATA PARTY

Skill: socialization

Materials:
* 2 paper plates
* markers, paints, paper scraps
* glue, stapler
* scissors, hole punch
* tissue paper strips
* string, long stick
* wrapped candy or treats
* rolled-up newspaper or plastic bat

Directions:

1. Staple two paper plates together ¾ of the way around. (The insides of the plates should be facing each other.)
2. Decorate the outside of the plates with markers or paints and paper scraps to resemble an animal or holiday character (for example: bunny, pumpkin, sun).
3. Glue on tissue paper strips.
4. Fill the inside with goodies, then staple the rest of the way around.
5. Punch a hole in the top and tie with string to a long stick.
6. Blindfold children (if desired) and let them swing at the moving piñata with a rolled-up newspaper or plastic bat.

Adaptations:

* Another easy piñata can be made with grocery bags. Double two grocery bags and fill with goodies. Fold the top half of the bag over the bottom of a hanger as illustrated and staple in place. Decorate with tissue paper and paint.
* Children can make individual piñatas with lunch bags.

295

CAMPING DAY

Skill: socialization

Materials:
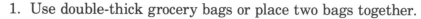
* grocery bags
* strips of fabric 2" × 24"
* scissors
* Velcro™

Directions:

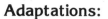

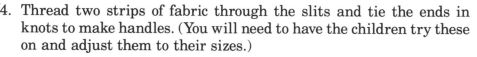

1. Use double-thick grocery bags or place two bags together.
2. Cut off three sides halfway down.
3. Cut four slits 2½" wide in the bag as shown.
4. Thread two strips of fabric through the slits and tie the ends in knots to make handles. (You will need to have the children try these on and adjust them to their sizes.)
5. Bring the top flap down and secure with a little strip of Velcro™.

Adaptations:

* Let the children decorate their backpacks with markers or crayons.
* Make trail mix or astronaut pudding to carry in your backpack.
* Set up a camping scene in your dramatic play area or outside with tents, camping equipment, etc.
* Ask parents to bring a tent and set it up on the playground for you.
* Let the children build the following tents:

   Drape a sheet over a table and secure the ends with rocks.

   Pin one end of a sheet to the fence. Secure the other end with rocks.

   Place two chairs back-to-back. Drape a sheet over the two chairs. Secure with rocks.

 **WILD WEST**

Skill: large-motor movement

Materials:
* lunch bags
* newspaper
* masking tape
* crayons or markers
* construction paper scraps

Directions:
1. Let children decorate lunch bags to look like pony heads. They may use markers, crayons, and construction paper scraps.
2. Take two sheets of newspaper and roll them lengthwise and tape. This will be the stick for your pony.
3. Tear another sheet of newspaper into strips and stuff into the sack for the pony's head.
4. Place the end of the bag over the newspaper roll and secure with tape.
5. Name your pony and "ride 'em pardner."

Adaptations:
* Serve baked beans, hot dogs, or trail mix for snack.
* Let the children make their own bandanas from solid fabric or cut-up old sheets. They can decorate their bandanas with markers or crayons, and they can create their own branding symbols.

OLYMPICS

Skill: large-motor movement

Materials:
* cardboard scraps
* aluminum foil
* hole punch
* red, white, and blue ribbon or yarn

Directions:

1. Cut cardboard in 4" circles and cover with aluminum foil.
2. Punch a hole in the medal, and string through yarn or ribbon to make a necklace.
3. Let the children participate in different events on the playground, such as throwing a Frisbee™, riding a tricycle, walking on the balance beam, running, kicking a ball, or throwing a beanbag at a target. (Encourage participation and avoid competition.)
4. Play some patriotic music. Then let the children stand on a drink crate or large block one at a time as you hang the medal around their necks.

Adaptations:

* Have opening ceremonies where children make paper flags and march around to music. Make a torch by wrapping a toilet paper dowel in aluminum foil and stuffing yellow cellophane paper in one end.
* Let children wear international dress and bring international foods to share for snack.

 **LUAU**

Skill: socialization

Materials:
* green drawstring garbage bags
* scissors
* yarn
* straws
* styrofoam egg cartons

Directions:

1. To make a grass skirt, cut off the bottom of the garbage bag. Starting at the bottom, cut 1½" strips in the bag. (Stop about 3" before you get to the drawstring.)
2. Pull the drawstring to fit the waist.
3. Cut straws into 1" pieces and string on yarn alternating with sections of the egg carton to make a lei. (Paper or tissue paper flowers can also be used.)

Adaptations:

* Serve pineapple, fruit kabobs, or other tropical delights for snack.
* Put on some Hawaiian music and try to hula.
* Make surf boards out of cardboard boxes and surf to some Beach Boys' music.
* Do the limbo!

CLOWN DAY

Skill: socialization

Materials:
* cornstarch
* cold cream
* red, yellow, and blue food coloring
* small cups, spoons
* cotton swabs

Directions:

1. Mix the following in three cups:

   1 tsp. cornstarch
   ½ tsp. water
   stir in ½ tsp. cold cream

2. Add a few drops food coloring to each cup.
3. Apply the face paint with your finger or cotton swab.

Adaptations:

* Make green, orange, and purple face paint by mixing the primary colors.
* Decorate a large paper grocery bag to look like a clown costume. Cut a large hole in the bottom of the bag for the head and smaller holes in the sides for arms.
* To make a clown collar, take the rim of a paper plate and glue crumbled tissue paper to it.
* Do stunts, tricks, and silly things to make each other laugh.
* Make funny face sandwiches or decorate cookies to look like clowns.

© 1994 by The Center for Applied Research in Education

HAPPY BIRTHDAY

Skill: self-esteem

Materials:
* * old cookie tin
* * Ivory™ Snowflake detergent
* * pan, spoon, water
* * birthday candles

Directions:

1. Pour 2 to 3 cups of Ivory™ flakes into the pan. Add just enough water to beat the flakes into a fluffy consistency (similar to icing).
2. Apply the flakes like icing around the sides and top of the pan. (Do not apply to the rim where the top fits down.)
3. Take the number of candles that will best represent the birthday your children will be celebrating in your room and put them on the top. (Build up the icing around them to hold them in place.)
4. Allow to dry overnight.
5. Place small toys, trinkets, and other goodies inside the cookie tin, then put on the top.
6. When someone has a birthday, light the candles, sing to them, and let them blow out the candles and make a wish. The birthday boy or girl may then look inside the "cake" and select a surprise.

Adaptations:

* * Let classmates write the birthday child a letter or draw them a picture. Put the pages together to make a "Birthday Book."
* * Instead of bringing sweets for their birthday, encourage parents to bring their child's favorite food, such as pizza, carrots and dip, corn on the cob, or whatever else.
* * Let the birthday child give a book, game, or other toy to the classroom on his or her birthday.
* * Make a paper crown, decorate their chair or desk, let them skip a written assignment, or think of other special ways to make the children feel "special" on their birthday.

RESOURCES

Ard, L., and Pitts, M., eds. *Room to Grow: How to Create Quality Early Childhood Environments.* Austin, TX: TAEYC, 1990.

Baratta-Lorton, M. *Mathematics Their Way.* Menlo Park, CA: Addison-Wesley, 1976.

Baratta-Lorton, M. *Workjobs.* Menlo Park, CA: Addison-Wesley, 1972.

Bos, G. *Please Don't Move the Muffin Tins.* Carmichael, CA: The Burton Gallery, 1978.

Brashears, D. *Dribble Drabble Art Experiences for Young Children.* Fort Collins, CO: DMC Publications, 1985.

Calvarese, J., and Sundman, C. *Year-Round Developmental Activities for Preschool Children.* West Nyack, NY: The Center for Applied Research in Education, 1990.

Coletta, A., and Coletta, K. *Year-Round Activities for Four-Year-Old Children.* West Nyack, NY: The Center for Applied Research in Education, 1986.

Croft, D., and Hess, R. *An Activities Handbook for Teachers of Young Children.* Boston: Houghton Mifflin, 1986.

Eisenhart, C., and Bell, R. *Pocketful of Miracles.* Livonia, MI: Partner Press, 1985.

Evans, J., and Moore, J. *How to Make Books with Children.* Carmel, CA: Evan-Moor, 1985.

Flemming, B., Hamilton, D., and Hicks, J. *Resources for Teaching in Early Childhood Education.* San Diego: Harcourt Brace Jovanovich, 1977.

Frank, M. *I Can Make a Rainbow.* Nashville: Incentive Publications, 1976.

Frost, J., and Klein, B. *Children's Play and Playgrounds.* Austin, TX: Playgrounds International, 1983.

Gilbert, L. *I Can Do It! I Can Do It!* Mt. Rainier, MD: Gryphon House, 1984.

Greenman, J. *Caring Spaces, Learning Places: Children's Environments That Work.* Redmond, WA: Exchange Press, 1989.

Gregson, B. *The Incredible Indoor Games Book.* Belmont, CA: David S. Lake, 1982.

Gregson, B. *The Outrageous Outdoor Games Book.* Belmont, CA: David S. Lake, 1982.

Harris, F. *Great Games to Play with Groups.* Carthage, IL: Fearon Teacher Aids, 1990.

Herr, J., and Libby, Y. *Creative Resources for the Early Childhood Classroom.* Albany, NY: Delmar, 1990.

Kamiya, A. *Elementary Teacher's Handbook of Indoor and Outdoor Games.* West Nyack, NY: Parker Publishing Company, 1985.

Kohl, M. *Scribble Cookies.* Bellingham, WA: Bright Ring, 1985.

Miller, K. *The Outside Play and Learning Book.* Mt. Rainier, MD: Gryphon House, 1988.

Mitchell, G., and Chemela, H. *I Am! I Can!* Mt. Rainier, MD: Gryphon House, 1987.

Patillo, J., and Vaughan, E. *Learning Centers for Child-Centered Classrooms.* Washington, D.C.: NEA, 1992.

Sanford, A., Williams, M., Jermes, J., and Overton, A. *A Planning Guide to the Preschool Curriculum.* Winston-Salem, NC: Kaplan, 1983.

Schickedanz, J. *More Than the ABC's: The Early Stages of Reading and Writing.* Washington, D.C.: NAEYC, 1990.

Schiller, P., and Rossano, J. *The Instant Curriculum.* Mt. Rainier, MD: Gryphon House, 1990.

Schirrmacher, R. *Art and Creative Development for Young Children.* Albany, NY: Delmar, 1988.

Schlosser, K., and Phillips, V. *Beginning in Whole Language.* New York: Scholastic, 1991.

Stassevitch, V., Stemmler, P., Shotwell, R., and Wirth, M. *Ready-to-Use Activities for Before and After School Programs.* West Nyack, NY: The Center for Applied Research in Education, 1989.

Stavros, S., and Peters, L. *Big Learning for Little Learners.* Mt. Rainier, MD: Gryphon House, 1987.

Stull, E., and Price, C. *Kindergarten Teacher's Month-by-Month Activities Program.* West Nyack, NY: The Center for Applied Research in Education, 1987.

Totline Staff. *1001 Teaching Props.* Everett, WA: Warren Publishing House, 1992.

Trister-Dodge, D. *The Creative Curriculum for Early Childhood.* Washington, D.C.: Teaching Strategies, 1988.

Warren, J. *1, 2, 3 Games.* Everett, WA: Totline Press, 1986.

Warren, J. *Theme-a-Saurus.* Everett, WA: Warren Publishing, 1990.

Williams, R., Rockwell, R., and Sherwood, E. *Mudpies to Magnets.* Mt. Rainier, MD: Gryphon House, 1987.

Wilmes, L., and Wilmes, D. *Learning Centers.* Elgin, IL: Building Blocks, 1991.